Project Maths

Text & Tests 1
Practice Book

Common Introductory Course
for First-Year Maths

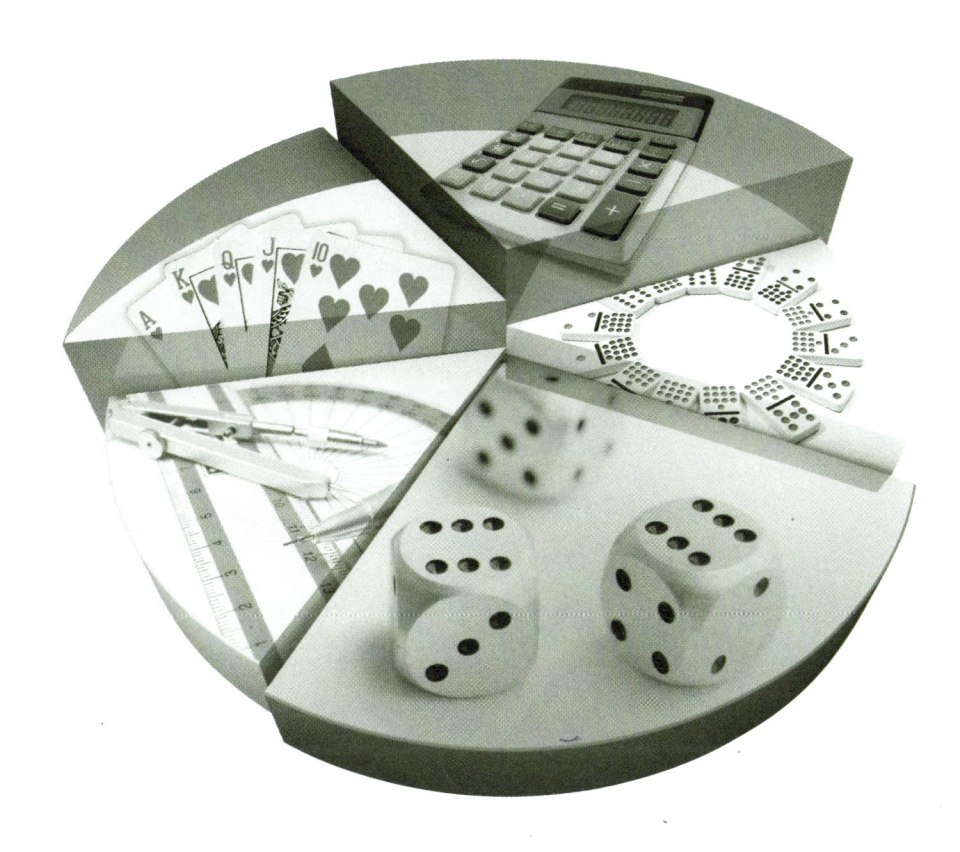

Paul Cooke

The Celtic Press

© Paul Cooke 2011

All rights reserved. No part of this publication may be reproduced, stored in a retrieval system or transmitted in any form or by any means, electronic, mechanical, photocopying, recording or otherwise, without the prior written consent of the copyright holders.

First published in 2011 by
The Celtic Press
Ground Floor – Block B
Liffey Valley Office Campus
Dublin 22.

This reprint August 2014

ISBN: 978-1-907705-13-7

Layout and artwork: Tech-Set Limited
Cover: Identikit Design

Printed and bound in Ireland by
W & G Baird
Caulside Drive
Antrim BT41 2RS

Preface

Text & Tests 1 Practice Book is a series of graded exercises compiled and written for **Project Maths – Common Introductory Course** for first-year students. It consolidates the material and topics covered in the textbook. It provides plenty of practice in the basic skills of mathematics in a directed and structured way. All the topics mentioned in the **Common Introductory Course** are included in the practice book.

Competence in the basic skills will lead to confidence and so develop in the student a sense of achievement and eliminate the 'fear factor' of maths. The step-by-step approach will help develop the student as a learner and encourage the move towards self-directed learning. The structure of the practice book helps the student in the proper layout of work and so become familiar with the desired steps and procedures.

This Practice Book can be used with any textbook.

Paul Cooke

Contents

Note: *** indicates slightly more challenging questions

1.1	**Natural Numbers**		5.7	Universal Set-Complement of a Set
1.2	Sets of Divisors		5.8	Venn Diagrams I
1.3	Primes		5.9	Venn Diagrams II
1.4	Multiples		5.10	Venn Diagrams III
1.5	Numbers/multiples/sequences		5.11	Cardinal Number (#)
1.6	Operations with Natural numbers		6.1	**Algebra**
1.7	Rounding Numbers		6.2	Evaluation of Expressions
1.8	Estimating		6.3	Forming Number Sentences
1.9	Index form		6.4	Solving Equations
1.10	Problems		7.1	**Perimeter and Area**
2.1	**Integers**		7.2	Area of Triangles
2.2	Multiplication and Division of Integers		7.3	Challenging Area/Perimeter Questions
2.3	Index form		8.1	**Proportion**
2.4	Integers: Order		8.2	Direct Proportion
2.5	Rounding Integers		8.3	Ratio
3.1	**Rational Numbers: Decimals – Fractions – Percentages**		8.4	Changing Ratios to Proportions
3.2	Adding and Subtracting Fractions		9.1	**Angles**
3.3	Multiplying and Dividing Fractions		9.2	Geometry I
3.4	BOMDAS and Fractions		9.3	Geometry II
3.5	Fraction Problems		9.4	Geometry III
3.6	Percentages/Fractions		10.1	**Statistics – Collecting data**
4.1	**Significant Figures**		10.2	Statistics – Types of data
4.2	Using Your Calculator		10.3	Statistics – Graphical methods
4.3	Number Lines		11.1	**Counting**
4.4	Commutative Property		11.2	The Fundamental Principle of Counting
4.5	Associative Property		11.3	Probability
4.6	Distributive Property		12.1	**Co-ordinate Geometry**
4.7	BOMDAS (Revision) II		12.2	Vertex – Edge – Face
4.8	Order of Operations III		12.3	Axial Symmetry/Central Symmetry
5.1	**Element of $\in$, Not an Element of $\notin$**		12.4	Experiments in Reflections
5.2	Listing the elements in a set		12.5	Geometry IV
5.3	Sets defined by a rule		12.6	Geometry V
5.4	Subset/Not a Subset		12.7	Geometry VI
5.5	Equality of sets		13.1	**Algebra & Patterns**
5.6	Union and Intersection of Sets			

1.1 Natural Numbers

The set of natural numbers is, N = {1, 2, 3, 4, 5, 6, ...}

1. Write TRUE or FALSE after each of the following.

(a) $6 \in N$ — T
(b) $-4 \in N$ — F
(c) $0 \in N$ — F
(d) $\frac{3}{4} \in N$ — F
(e) $2.5 \in N$ — F
(f) $3 \notin N$ — F
(g) $-7 \notin N$ — T
(h) $25 \in N$ — T
(i) $125 \in N$ — T
(j) $70 \notin N$ — F
(k) $7 \in N$ — T
(l) $3\frac{1}{3} \notin N$ — T
(m) $5967 \in N$ — T
(n) $345.5 \in N$ — F
(o) $0.01 \notin N$ — T

2. Place the symbols $<$ or $>$ between each of the following pairs of numbers.

(i) $6 > 4$
(ii) $6 < 10$
(iii) $10 > 6$
(iv) $4 < 5$
(v) $116 > 3$
(vi) $36 > 30$
(vii) $80 < 180$
(viii) $2 < 3$

Remember:
$a > b$, a is greater than b
$a < b$, a is less than b

Example: Find the values of $x \in N$, in each of the following.

(a) $3 < x \leq 6$ answer $x = 4, 5, 6$
(b) $x \leq 4$ answer $x = 1, 2, 3, 4$
(c) $3 \leq x$ answer $x = 3, 4, 5, 6, ...$

Remember:
$a \geq b$, a is greater than or equal to b
$a \leq b$, a is less than or equal to b

3. If $x \in N$, find each of the following.

(a) $2 < x < 8$ answer $x = 3, 4, 5, 6$
(b) $3 \leq x < 6$ answer $x = 3, 4, 5$
(c) $x < 5$ answer $x = 1, 2, 3, 4$
(d) $10 \leq x \leq 13$ answer $x = 10, 11, 12, 13$
(e) $x \geq 4$ answer $x = 1, 2, 3$ and 4
(f) $6 < x$ answer $x = 7, 8 ...$
(g) $4 < x < 6$ answer $x = 5$
(h) $9 \leq x \leq 15$ answer $x = 9, 10, 11, 12, 13, 14, 15$
(i) $1 < x \leq 7$ answer $x = 2, 3, 4, 5, 6, 7$
(j) $25 \leq x < 30$ answer $x = 25, 26, 27, 28, 29$
(k) $10 \geq x > 5$ answer $x = 10, 9, 8, 7, 6$
(l) $3 \geq x$ answer $x = 3, 2, 1$
(m) $12 > x > 9$ answer $x = 11, 10$
(n) $x \geq 2$ answer $x = 2, 3 ...$

Date 21/9/16   Signed ....

4. Write each of the following in order, starting with the smallest.
   (a) 604, 406, 64, 46, 0   0, 46, 64, 406, 604
   (b) 210, 85, 219, 26, 401, 79, 151   26, 79, 85, 151, 210, 219, 401
   (c) 755, 745, 754, 744   744, 745, 754, 755
   (d) 3601, 3061, 1630, 6103, 6103   1630, 3061, 3601, 6103

5. Given that 2176 = 2000 + 100 + 70 + 6, write the value of each of the underlined digits.
   (a) 3<u>4</u>8 = 40   (b) <u>2</u>674 = 2,000   (c) 79<u>9</u> = 9
   (d) 267<u>1</u> = 1   (e) <u>8</u>18 = 800   (f) <u>9</u>2 = 90
   (g) <u>1</u>3674 = 10,000   (h) 2<u>5</u>999 = 5,000   (i) <u>8</u>1818 = 80,000

6. Write the following numbers in words.
   (a) 187   One hundred and eighty seven
   (b) 201   Two hundred and one
   (c) 3045   Three thousand and forty five
   (d) 7001   Seven thousand and one
   (e) 8203   Eight thousand, two hundred and three
   (f) 11459   Eleven thousand, four hundred and fifty nine
   (g) 20703   Twenty thousand, seven hundred and three

7. Write the following numbers in figures.
   (a) seven thousand and twenty six   7,026
   (b) eight hundred and seventeen   817
   (c) one thousand and ten   1,010
   (d) eighty thousand, three hundred and five   80,305
   (e) one million, three hundred thousand and forty one   1,300,041
   (f) two million, thirteen thousand and thirty one   2,013,013 31
   (g) four hundred and fifty nine thousand and seventy two   459,072

Well done

Date 21/9/16   Signed

8. List the natural numbers in each of the following.

(a) The even numbers between 5 and 13.

(b) The odd numbers between 4 and 11.

(c) The odd numbers between 5 and 17.

(d) The even numbers between 9 and 12 inclusive.

(e) The next five even numbers greater than 7.

(f) The next four odd numbers greater than 13.

9. Using the number of digits indicated in the brackets (each digit used only once), write the largest and smallest number possible. (zero cannot be the first digit!)

			Largest	Smallest
(a)	(3)	4, 1, 6, 7, 3, 9.	976	134
(b)	(2)	8, 1, 9, 5, 0, 4.		
(c)	(4)	3, 0, 4, 5, 6, 1, 2.		
(d)	(3)	8, 3, 7, 6, 4, 1, 9.		
(e)	(5)	3, 7, 1, 8, 4, 9, 0, 2.		
(f)	(3)	2, 9, 3, 8, 0.		
(g)	(4)	1, 9, 7, 8, 0.		
(h)	(3)	2, 5, 1, 0, 6.		
(i)	(4)	4, 3, 7, 0, 1, 2.		
(j)	(3)	6, 8, 0, 4, 2, 1, 9.		
(k)	(3)	3, 9, 3, 3, 0.		
(l)	(4)	1, 0, 7, 0, 0.		
(m)	(3)	0, 5, 9.		
(n)	(4)	8, 6, 7, 9, 1, 8.		
(o)	(4)	3, 0, 7, 0.		
(p)	(2)	1, 0, 7, 8, 9.		
(q)	(5)	1, 6, 0, 5, 9.		
(r)	(4)	8, 1, 1, 9, 1, 1.		
(s)	(3)	4, 5, 6, 7, 7.		
(t)	(4)	1, 2, 9, 6, 5.		
(u)	(2)	3, 7, 0, 1.		
(v)	(3)	5, 5, 7, 7, 8.		
(w)	(4)	9, 0, 1, 2, 3.		
(x)	(3)	3, 9, 4, 3, 8, 5.		

Date .... Signed ....

1.2 Sets of Divisors

Example: Find all the divisors of 15

The divisors of 15 are (1, 3, 5, 15)

Make a list of all the divisors of each of the following numbers.

	Number	Divisors		Number	Divisors
1.	8		9.	11	
2.	10		10.	34	
3.	9		11.	18	
4.	14		12.	30	
5.	32		13.	31	
6.	35		14.	21	
7.	28		15.	19	
8.	44		16.	52	

Example: Find pairs of factors for 15.

The factor pairs are (1, 15), (3, 5)

Make a list of all the factor pairs of each of the following numbers

	Number	Factor pairs		Number	Factor pairs
1.	40		11.	19	
2.	35		12.	23	
3.	36		13.	44	
4.	16		14.	28	
5.	38		15.	15	
6.	45		16.	13	
7.	56		17.	12	
8.	50		18.	29	
9.	27		19.	123	
10.	18		20.	100	

Date .... Signed ....

1.3 Primes

> A prime number is a number that only has one and itself as divisors.
> i.e. if a is prime, then $(1, a)$ are the only factors.

Find all the prime numbers in each of the following ranges of numbers.

1. Between 0–10
2. Between 10–20
3. Between 20–30
4. Between 30–40
5. Between 40–50
6. Between 50–60
7. Between 60–70
8. Between 70–80
9. Between 80–90
10. Between 90–100

1.4 Multiples

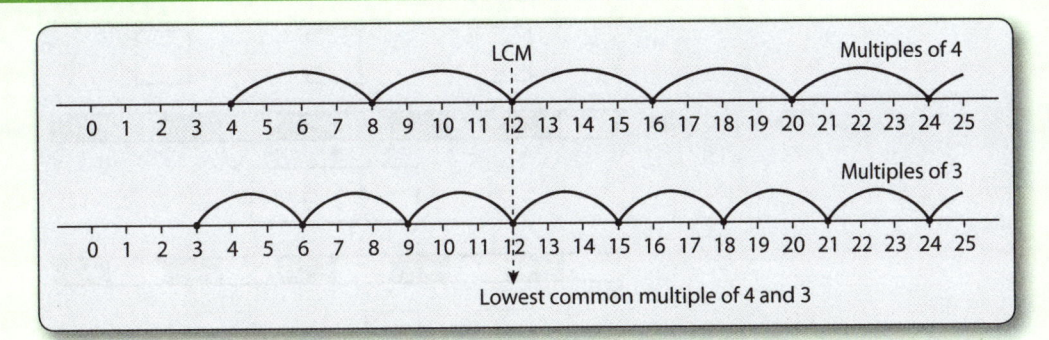

Find the lowest common multiple of each of the following pairs of numbers.

Multiples   LCM

1. 3 ;
   5 ;

2. 2 ;
   7 ;

3. 4 ;
   6 ;

4. 20 ;
   30 ;

5. 5 ;
   15 ;

6. 4 ;
   5 ;

7. 12 ;
   15 ;

8. 24 ;
   30 ;

Date ....   Signed ....

1.5 Numbers/multiples/sequences

1. Examine closely the following number sticks. The first and last number is given. In each box provided, write the number that is missing

   Rough work

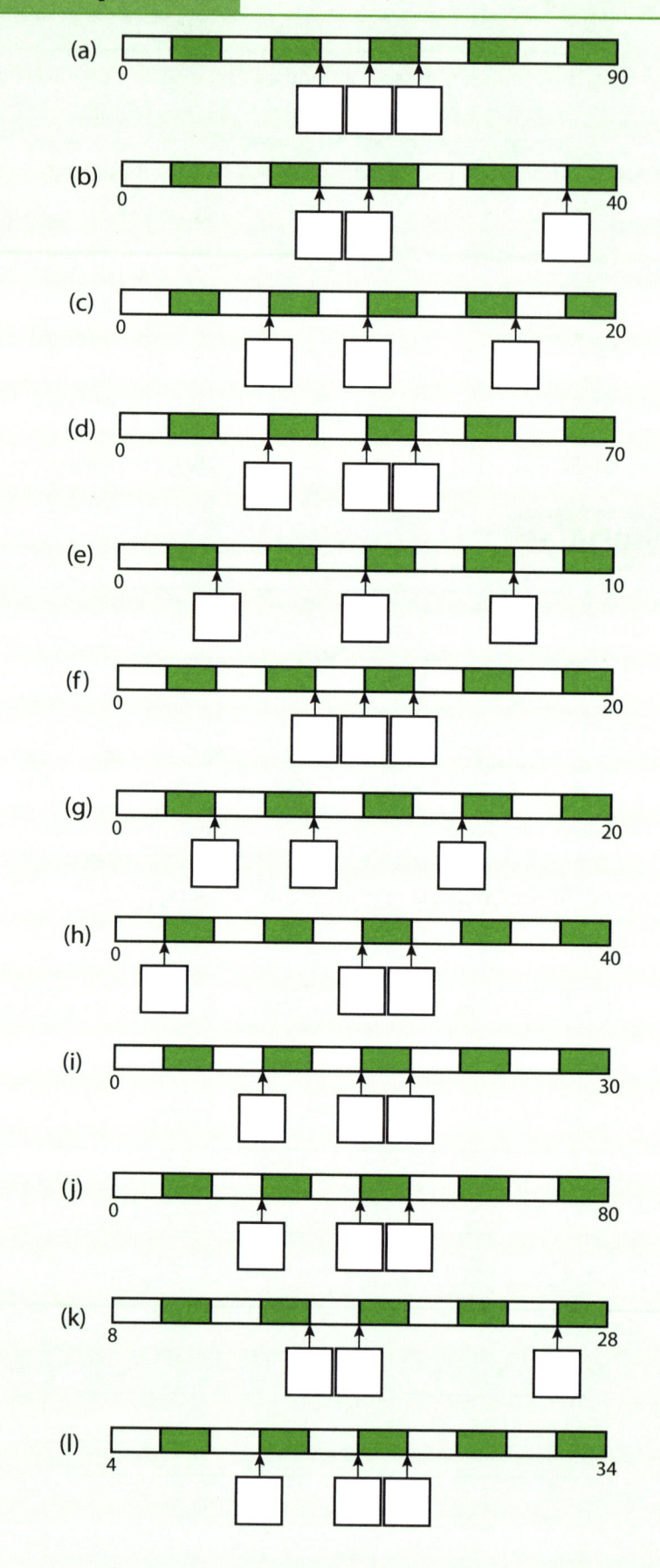

(a) 0 — 90

(b) 0 — 40

(c) 0 — 20

(d) 0 — 70

(e) 0 — 10

(f) 0 — 20

(g) 0 — 20

(h) 0 — 40

(i) 0 — 30

(j) 0 — 80

(k) 8 — 28

(l) 4 — 34

Date .... Signed ....

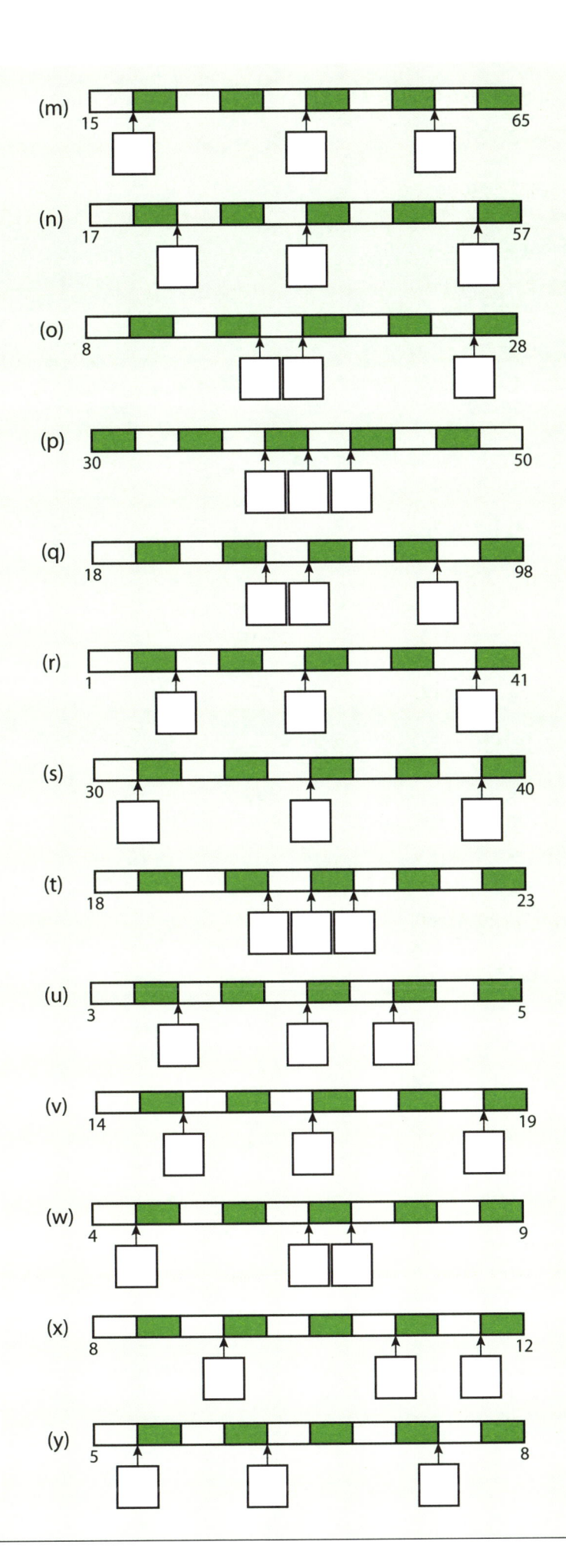

Rough work

2. Insert the missing numbers in each of the following sequences.   Rough work

   (i) 7, 14, 21, 28, 35,   ,   , 56,

   (ii) 8, 15, 22, 29, 36,   ,   , 57,

   (iii) 5, 8, 11, 14, 17,   ,   , 26,

   (iv) 17, 22, 27, 32,   ,   , 47,   ,

   (v) 5, 14, 23, 32, 41,   ,   , 68,

   (vi) 7, 11, 15, 19,   ,   , 31,   ,

   (vii) 12, 17, 22,   ,   , 37, 42,   ,

3. (i) $-3, -1, 1, 3, 5, 7,$,   ,

   (ii) $-2, 0, 2, 4, 6,$,   , 12,

   (iii) $-4, -6, -8, -10,$,   , $-16,$

   (iv) $-1, -5, -9, -13,$,   , $-25,$

   (v) 4, 7, 10, 13,   ,   , 22,

   (vi) $-4, 1, 6, 11,$,   ,   , 31

   (vii) $-3, -4, -5,$,   , $-8,$,

4. (i) 5, 10, 18, 29, 43, 60,   ,   ,

   (ii) 2, 3, 6, 11, 18,   ,   ,

   (iii) 8, 4, 2, 1,   ,   ,

   (iv) $-3, 6, -12, 24, -48,$,   ,

   (v) 2, 3, 5, 9, 17,   ,   ,

   (vi) 1, 3, 9, 27,   ,   ,

   (vii) 5, 7, 10, 14,   ,   ,

   (viii) 2, 1, 3, 4, 7,   ,   ,

   (ix) 4, 5, 3, 6, 2,   ,   ,

   (x) $1, \frac{1}{4}, \frac{1}{7}, \frac{1}{10},$,   ,

Date ....   Signed ....

1.6 Operations with Natural numbers

Without using a calculator, find the missing natural number in each of the following (using a note pad where necessary).

1. $1 + 8 =$
2. $15 - 6 =$
3. $6 \times 2 =$
4. $30 \div 5 =$

5. $35 + 26 =$
6. $38 - 32 =$
7. $5 \times 17 =$
8. $49 \div 7 =$

9. $56 + 54 =$
10. $70 - 33 =$
11. $3 \times 22 =$
12. $108 \div 9 =$

13. $76 + 89 =$
14. $87 - 75 =$
15. $6 \times 32 =$
16. $153 \div 9 =$

17. $\_\_ + 18 = 41$
18. $6 - \_\_ = 0$
19. $3 \times \_\_ = 24$
20. $12 \div \_\_ = 3$

21. $61 + \_\_ = 116$
22. $62 - \_\_ = 53$
23. $\_\_ \times 28 = 140$
24. $\_\_ \div 6 = 15$

25. $86 + \_\_ = 166$
26. $\_\_ - 46 = 43$
27. $\_\_ \times 4 = 124$
28. $68 \div \_\_ = 17$

29. $23 + \_\_ = 46$
30. $\_\_ \div 6 = 1$
31. $10 \times \_\_ = 80$
32. $\_\_ - 12 = 35$

33. Complete the following magic squares. Each row, column and diagonal must add up to the <u>total given</u>.

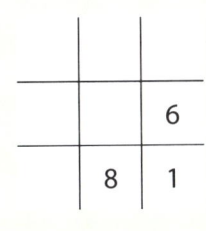

	6	
8	1	

Total 12

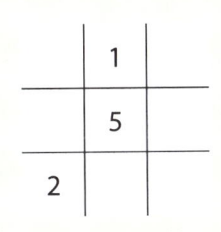

	1	
	5	
2		

Total 15

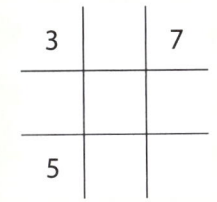

3		7
5		

Total 18

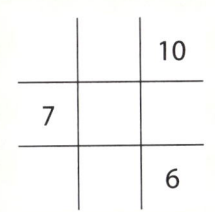

		10
7		
		6

Total 27

34. Complete the following magic squares. Each row, column and diagonal must add up to the <u>same total</u>.

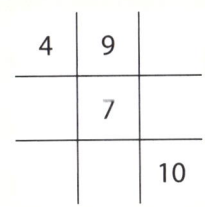

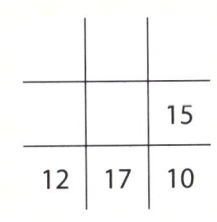

4	9	
	7	
		10

		15
12	17	10

	14	21	
	20	9	
		10	12
22			11

Date .... Signed ....

31. Complete the following number triangles. A number must equal the total of the two numbers that it rests on.

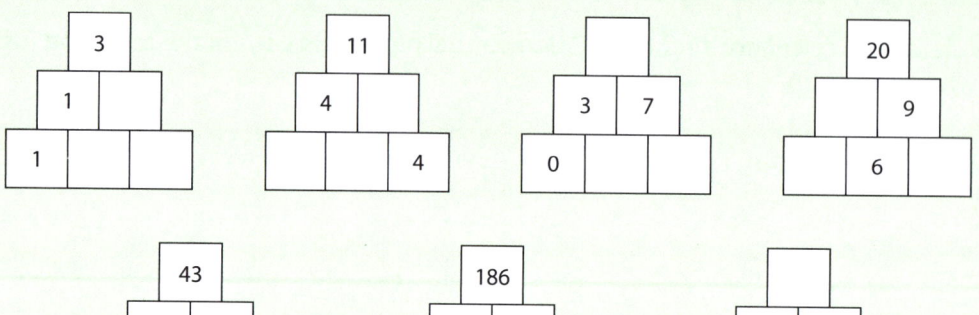

Triangle 1: top 3, middle row: 1, _; bottom row: 1, _, _

Triangle 2: top 11, middle row: 4, _; bottom row: _, 4, _

Triangle 3: top _, middle row: 3, 7; bottom row: 0, _, _

Triangle 4: top 20, middle row: _, 9; bottom row: 6, _, _

32.

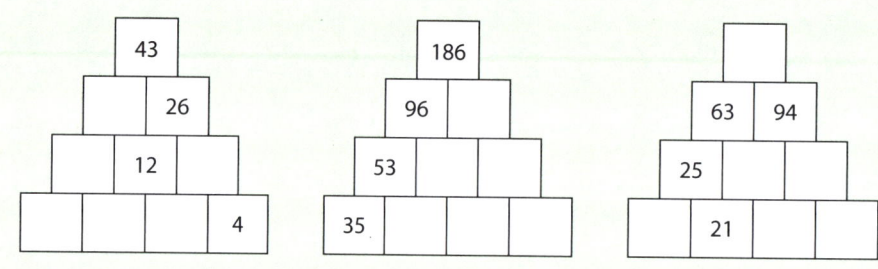

Triangle 1: top 43, next 26, next 12, bottom ends with 4

Triangle 2: top 186, next 96, next 53, bottom starts with 35

Triangle 3: top _, next 63, 94; next 25, _, _; bottom 21, _, _

33. A man wins €55,120 in prize money. He shares the prize equally between himself and his 7 team mates. How much does each person receive?

34. A hall has 12 rows each with 18 seats. How many seats are in the hall altogether?

35. The population of a town changed from 60,000 to 43,000. How many people left the town?

36. A €380,000 house decreased in value by €102,000. What is it worth now?

37. Fence posts are 3 m apart. If a fence is made of 10 posts, how long is the fence?

38. One costs 13c, five costs 65c. How much would 104 cost?

39. There are 24 more boys than girls in a school of 404 students. How many girls are there?

40. A building has 12 floors each 4 m high and a roof 5 m high. How tall is the building?

41. Alice saves €2 each weekday and €5 each Saturday and Sunday for 8 weeks. How much has she saved in total?

42. Each hour a spider climbs 30 cm up a wall 2.8 m high and falls back down 10 cm. How long will it take the spider to fully climb the wall?

Date .... Signed ....

1.7 Rounding Numbers

Example: Round (a) 134 to the nearest 10 → 130

Round (b) 2099 to the nearest 100 → 2100

Round each of the following to the number given. If a number ends with 5, round up.

1. To the nearest 10

63 →
33 →
12 →
331 →
86 →
28 →
45 →
114 →
207 →
638 →
297 →
1245 →
7 →
445 →
618 →
391 →
1003 →
210 →
555 →
1999 →

2. To the nearest 100

163 →
181 →
1505 →
472 →
1862 →
444 →
191 →
844 →
1599 →
1348 →
1222 →
97 →
124 →
58 →
1717 →
182 →
128 →
3929 →
525 →
47 →

3. To the nearest 1000

2310 →
4250 →
33,100 →
41,900 →
3870 →
11,565 →
40,390 →
6570 →
19,620 →
2400 →
2450 →
7150 →
13,600 →
43,700 →
9250 →
13,190 →
27,610 →
113,400 →
129,700 →
340 →

Date .... Signed ....

1.8 Estimating

Example: Estimate the value of $\frac{48 \times 73}{136}$ by rounding each number to the nearest 10.

Answer
$\frac{48 \times 73}{136} \rightarrow \frac{50 \times 70^1}{140_2} = 25$

Estimate the value of each of the following by rounding to the nearest 10 first.

1. $\frac{19 \times 57}{63} \rightarrow$ =
2. $\frac{56 \times 111}{24} \rightarrow$ =
3. $\frac{38 \times 76}{42} \rightarrow$ =
4. $\frac{88 \times 27}{58} \rightarrow$ =
5. $\frac{90 \times 98}{63} \rightarrow$ =
6. $\frac{146 \times 29}{53} \rightarrow$ =
7. $\frac{195 \times 78}{157} \rightarrow$ =
8. $\frac{23 \times 55}{44 \times 44} \rightarrow$ =
9. $\frac{134}{21 \times 258} \rightarrow$ =
10. $\frac{39 \times 54}{46 \times 44} \rightarrow$ =
11. $\frac{374 \times 49}{14 \times 365} \rightarrow$ =
12. $\frac{31 \times 49}{145} \rightarrow$ =

Without using a calculator, find the value of each of the following.

1. $\sqrt{25} =$
2. $\sqrt{36} =$
3. $\sqrt{49} =$
4. $\sqrt{1} =$
5. $\sqrt{121} =$
6. $\sqrt{64} =$
7. $\sqrt{16} =$
8. $\sqrt{100} =$
9. $\sqrt{81} =$
10. $8^2 =$
11. $\sqrt{144} =$
12. $7^2 =$
13. $4^2 =$
14. $13^2 =$
15. $\sqrt{225} =$
16. $\sqrt{4} =$
17. $6^2 =$
18. $\sqrt{625} =$ ***
19. $5^2 =$
20. $9^2 =$
21. $\sqrt{9} =$
22. $7^2 =$
23. $\sqrt{4^2} =$
24. $\sqrt{6^2} =$

Date .... Signed ....

1.9 Index form… a^n, $a \in \mathbb{N}$

(i) $3 \times 3 \times 3 \times 3 = 3^4$ (3 to the power of 4)
(ii) $3 \times 3 \times 3 \times 5 \times 5 = 3^3 \times 5^2$ (3 to the power of 3 multiplied by 5 to the power of 2)

Write each of the following in index form.

1. $2 \times 2 \times 2 \times 2 \times 2 =$

2. $4 \times 4 \times 4 =$

3. $6 \times 6 \times 6 \times 6 =$

4. $5 \times 5 \times 5 \times 3 \times 3 \times 3 =$

5. $7 \times 7 \times 2 \times 2 \times 2 \times 2 =$

6. $8 \times 8 \times 8 \times 5 \times 5 \times 5 \times 5 =$

7. $9 \times 9 \times 2 \times 2 \times 2 \times 2 \times 2 =$

8. $\dfrac{6 \times 6 \times 6}{4 \times 4 \times 4 \times 4} =$

9. $\dfrac{7 \times 7 \times 7 \times 2 \times 2}{3 \times 3 \times 3 \times 3} =$ ***

Example: Simplify (a) $3^4 \times 3^2$ $= 3^6$
(b) $\dfrac{4^5}{4^2}$ $= 4^3$

Simplify each of the following.

1. $4^3 \times 4^4 =$ 4^7
2. $7^5 \times 7^2 =$
3. $3^2 \times 3^5 =$
4. $8^3 \times 8^2 =$
5. $c^7 \times c^5 =$ ***
6. $\dfrac{5^6}{5^2} =$ 5^4
7. $\dfrac{3^4}{3^3} =$
8. $\dfrac{6^7}{6^6} =$
9. $\dfrac{2^{10}}{2^7} =$
10. $\dfrac{5^9}{5^1} =$
11. $\dfrac{b^7}{b^5} =$ ***

12. $6^2 \times 6^3 =$
13. $8^3 \times 8^3 =$
14. $5^6 \times 5^3 \times 5^2 =$
15. $7^2 \times 7^4 \times 7^6 =$
16. $3^9 \times 3^6 =$
17. $\dfrac{2^{10}}{2^5} =$
18. $\dfrac{8^5}{8^2} =$
19. $\dfrac{7^8}{7^8} =$
20. $\dfrac{12^5}{12^2} =$
21. $\dfrac{8^3}{8^7} =$ ***
22. $\dfrac{20^6}{20^5} =$

23. $\dfrac{8^4}{8^3} =$
24. $\dfrac{9^7}{9^4} =$
25. $\dfrac{7^7}{7^4} =$
26. $\dfrac{2^{16}}{2^{12}} =$
27. $4^6 \times 4^5 =$
28. $\dfrac{8^{10}}{8^6} =$
29. $2^4 \times 2^3 \times 2^5 =$
30. $\dfrac{4^6}{4^5} =$
31. $7^2 \times 7^6 =$
32. $9^2 \times 9^6 =$
33. $\dfrac{9^2}{9^6} =$ ***

Date .... Signed ....

Simplify each of the following, giving your answer in index form.

Remember: $a^0 = 1, a \in R$

1. $\dfrac{5^4 \times 5^3}{5^2} =$ $\dfrac{5^7}{5^2} = 5^5$

2. $\dfrac{3^4 \times 3^5}{3^3} =$

3. $\dfrac{4^7 \times 4^2}{4^2} =$

4. $\dfrac{b^2 \times b^5}{b^3 \times b^4} =$

5. $\dfrac{3^9 \times 3^6}{3^3 \times 3^7} =$

6. $\dfrac{4^{10} \times 4^{12}}{4^7 \times 4^{11}} =$

7. $\dfrac{3^9 \times 3^6}{3^3 \times 3^7} =$

8. $\dfrac{4^8 \times 4^9}{4^5 \times 4^7} =$

9. $\dfrac{7^2 \times 7^8}{7^3 \times 7^4} =$

10. $\dfrac{2^4 \times 2^6}{2^5 \times 2^2} =$

11. $\dfrac{6^2 \times 6^4 \times 6^3}{6^5 \times 6^2} =$

12. $\dfrac{2 \times 2^3 \times 2^6}{2^8} =$

13. $\dfrac{3^3 \times 3^3 \times 3^3}{3^2 \times 3^2} =$

14. $\dfrac{7^3 \times 7^3 \times 7^3}{7^2 \times 7^2} =$

15. $\dfrac{5^4 \times 5^3}{5^2 \times 5} =$

16. $\dfrac{a^6 \times a^4}{a^2} =$ $\dfrac{a^{(\ \ )}}{a^2} = a^{(\ \ )}$

17. $\dfrac{6^6 \times 6^5}{6^3} =$

18. $\dfrac{2^{10} \times 2^3}{2^7} =$

19. $\dfrac{2^8 \times 2^7}{2^4 \times 2^4} =$

20. $\dfrac{a^4 \times a^2}{a^3 \times a^1} =$

21. $\dfrac{2^{10} \times 2^3}{2^7 \times 2^4} =$

22. $\dfrac{6^4 \times 6^2}{6^3 \times 6^1} =$

23. $\dfrac{2^{10} \times 2^3}{2^3 \times 2^8} =$ ***

24. $\dfrac{5^6 \times 5^4}{5^3 \times 5^9} =$ ***

25. $\dfrac{6^{13}}{6^5 \times 6^5} =$

26. $\dfrac{8^7}{8^4 \times 8^3} =$

27. $\dfrac{3^4 \times 3^2 \times 3^5}{3^{11}} =$

28. $\dfrac{4^4 \times 4^8}{4^2 \times 4^6} =$

29. $\dfrac{7^5}{7^2} \times \dfrac{7^6}{7^4} =$

30. $\dfrac{6^6 \times 6^3}{6^4 \times 6^5} =$

Date ....   Signed ....

1.10 Problems (use a notepad where necessary)

1. Using the digits 5, 1, 3 and 9 in the number, find the difference between the largest and the smallest four digit number that can be made from these digits.

2. (a) List the first 10 prime numbers. = (,   ,   ,   ,   ,   ,   ,   ,   ,   )
   (b) Write the number 30 as
   (i) the sum of three prime numbers   =   +   +   = 30
   (ii) the product of three prime numbers   =   ×   ×   = 30

3. When a bus reaches a bus stop there were 34 passengers on board. If 8 people got on the bus and 12 got off, how many passengers where then on the bus?

4. Write the next two lines in the following number pattern.

   1^3 = 1 = 1^2

   $1^3 + 2^3$ = 9 = 3^2

   $1^3 + 2^3 + 3^3$ = 36 = 6^2

   =   =

   =   =

5. Which of the following has the greatest value?

   (A) $(1 \times 2) \times (3 \times 4)$ or   (B) $(1 \times 2) + (3 \times 4)$ or   (C) $(1 \times 2) \times (3 + 4)$ or
   (D) $(1 + 2) \times (3 \times 4)$ or   (E) $(1 + 2) \times (3 + 4)$

6. Four of the five options are equal. Which is the odd one out?

   (A) $1 \div 9 + 9 \div 1$ (B) $(1 \times 9 \div (9 \times 1)$ (C) $1 - 9 + 9 \times 1$
   (D) $1 + 9 \div 9 - 1$ (E) $1 \times (9 - 9) + 1$.

7. A gym has 69 members. 38 of the members are boys. There are 19 members who are girls under 15 years old. There are 23 members who are boys 15 yrs old or older.

	Under 15 yrs old	15 yrs or older	Totals
Boys		23	38
Girls	19		
Totals			69

   Complete the Two-way table.

   Date ....   Signed ....

2.1 Integers

Integers are positive and negative whole numbers.
$Z = \{\ldots -5, -4, -3, -2, -1, 0, 1, 2, 3, 4, 5, \ldots\}$

$(-) \leftarrow$ −11 −10 −9 −8 −7 −6 −5 −4 −3 −2 −1 0 1 2 3 4 5 6 7 8 9 10 11 $\rightarrow (+)$

1. Write these numbers in order of size, smallest first.
   (a) 4, 7, −3, 0, −2, −5
   (b) 6, −3, −9, 4, −4, 0
   (c) 0, 2, −1, −9, −3, −6
   (d) 4, −4, 1, −2, 3
   (e) 0, 3, −1, 4, −6

2. Use the symbols > and < to compare these pairs of numbers.
   (a) −6   −3
   (b) 0   −1
   (c) −7   −10
   (d) −31   −20
   (e) −1   8

Remember: Integers are directed numbers
+6 is → → → → → →
−3 is ← ← ←

3. Increase the following numbers by 6.
   (a) 7 →   (b) −2 →
   (c) 2 →   (d) −8 →
   (e) −1 →   (f) −6 →
   (g) −91 →   (h) −20 →

4. Decrease the following numbers by 5.
   (a) 12 →   (b) 0 →
   (c) −1 →   (d) 4 →
   (e) 3 →   (f) −49 →
   (g) 2 →   (h) −5 →

5. Find the value of each of the following.   **Remember:** −(−3) = +3

   (a) −7 + 3 + 1 =   (b) −9 + 5 + 7 =   (c) 4 + 5 − 2 =
   (d) −2 − 4 − 5 =   (e) 4 + 9 + 1 =   (f) −2 − 8 + 6 =
   (g) −8 − 6 + 9 =   (h) −3 + 4 − 9 =   (i) −1 − 1 − 2 =
   (j) −6 − (−2) + 1 =   (k) −4 − 3 − (−2) =   (l) 5 − 3 − (−2) =
   (m) +14 + 8 − 17 =   (n) −25 − (−10) − 5 = (o) −125 − (−75) =
   (p) 45 − (−18) − 7 =   (q) −35 + 17 − (−20) = (r) −75 − (−60) =

Date ....   Signed ....

2.2 Multiplication and Division of Integers

Remember:
$3 \times 5 = 15$ $3 \times -5 = -15$ $\frac{10}{2} = 5$ $\frac{-10}{2} = -5$

$-3 \times -5 = 15$ $-3 \times 5 = -15$ $\frac{-10}{-2} = 5$ $\frac{10}{-2} = -5$

Evaluate each of the following.

1. $6 \times 5 =$
2. $2 \times -5 =$
3. $9 \times (-3) =$
4. $8 \times 4 =$
5. $-6 \times (-5) =$
6. $-2 \times 4 =$
7. $9 \times -4 =$
8. $-4 \times (-4) =$
9. $-7 \times (-3) =$
10. $2 \times (-15) =$

11. $\frac{-4}{2} =$
12. $\frac{-12}{6} =$
13. $\frac{4}{-2} =$
14. $\frac{-18}{-2} =$
15. $\frac{-28}{7} =$
16. $\frac{36}{12} =$
17. $\frac{-14 + 16}{2} =$
18. $\frac{24 - 9}{5} =$
19. $\frac{14 - 38}{8} =$
20. $\frac{-8}{-8} =$

21. $\frac{4 \times 4}{2 \times (-2)} =$
22. $\frac{-3 \times 4}{2 \times 6} =$
23. $\frac{-6 \times (-4)}{-2 \times (-3)} =$
24. $\frac{2 \times (-4)}{-8} =$
25. $\frac{-4(3 - 6)}{7 - 1} =$
26. $\frac{-6(2 - 4)}{9 - 7} =$
27. $\frac{-10 \times (-5)}{8 - 3} =$
28. $\frac{-4(6 - 5)}{2 - 4} =$
29. $\frac{-10 + 5 + 15}{5} =$
30. $\frac{-3 \times (-4) \times 2}{1 + 2 + 3} =$

BOMDAS: Do what is in brackets; then multiply and divide before you add and subtract.

1. $(4 + 5) \times 3 - 2 \quad = 9 \times 3 - 2 \quad = 27 - 2 = 25$.

2. $3 + 2 \times (5 - 2) =$
3. $2 \times (3 - 5) + 6 =$
4. $3 \times (6 - 2) \times 4 =$
5. $2 - 4 \times (5 - 4) =$
6. $3 + 2 \times (4 - 5) =$

7. $2(4 + 5) - 3(7 - 1) =$
8. $3(4 + 2) - 2(5 - 2) =$
9. $5 \times (3 - 2) + 3 \times 4 =$
10. $6 \times 2 + 5 \times 4 \div 2 =$
11. $(4 - 6 + 3)(6 - 2 - 1) =$

Date ....   Signed ....

12. $36 - 14 \div 7 \times 3 =$

13. $(6 - 4)(5 - 2) =$

14. $-6 - (-2) - (-7) =$

15. $\dfrac{4(-2) + 3(16)}{2(6 + 4)} =$

16. $(4 - 6 + 3)(6 - 2 - 1) =$

17. $\dfrac{-5 + 2(-8)}{-11 + 4} =$

18. $\dfrac{5 + 2(-8)}{-4 - 7} =$

19. $\dfrac{3(2 + 4)}{2(7 - 4)} =$

20. $13 + \dfrac{4(2 - 11)}{3} =$

21. $\dfrac{16}{4} - \dfrac{2(9 - 3)}{4} =$

22. Insert brackets into each of the following to make the answer correct.

(a) $3 + 5 \times 6 = 48$ (b) $32 \div 2 + 6 = 4$ (c) $30 - 2 \times 3 + 1 = 22$

23. What is the difference between these night and day temperatures?

(a) night $-4\,°C$ day $6\,°C$

(b) night $-5\,°C$ day $0\,°C$

(c) night $-14\,°C$ day $-7\,°C$

(d) night $-9\,°C$ day $9\,°C$

(e) night $-10\,°C$ day $-1\,°C$

(f) night $-14\,°C$ day $-2\,°C$

24. Complete the magic squares.

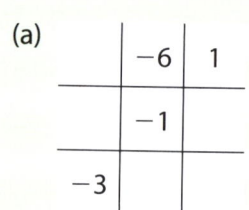

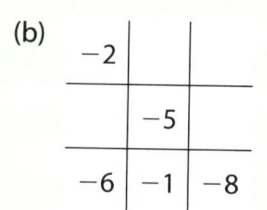

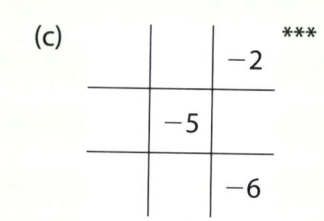

(a)
	-6	1
	-1	
-3		

(b)
-2		
	-5	
-6	-1	-8

(c) ***
		-2
	-5	
		-6

25. Complete the pyramid.

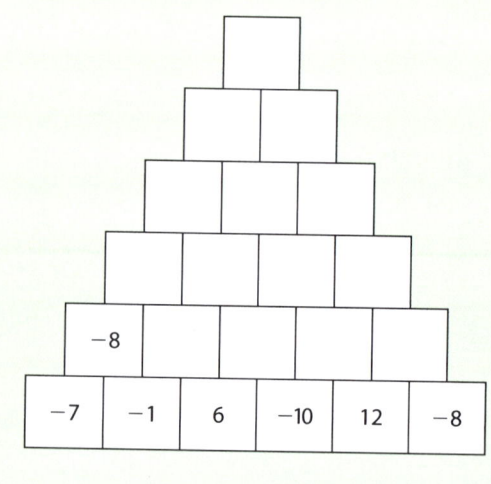

Bottom row: -7, -1, 6, -10, 12, -8

Second row from bottom leftmost: -8

26. Fill in the missing numbers.

(a) $4 - \square = -2$

(b) $-3 - \square = 3$

(c) $-5 + \square = -8$

(d) $11 - \square = 13$

(e) $-15 + \square = -4$

(f) $\square + 23 + \square = -5$

Date ....   Signed ....

27. Complete these upside-down pyramids using subtraction.
i.e. subtract the right hand number from the left hand number and write your answer below.

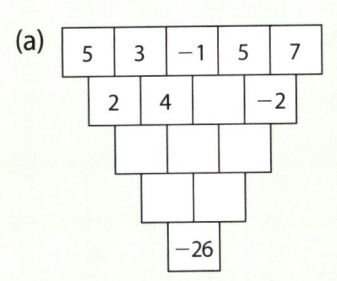

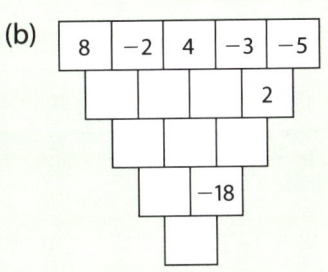

(a)
5	3	−1	5	7
2	4		−2
−26

(b)
8	−2	4	−3	−5
			2
	−18

28. Complete the following multiplication grid.

×	−2		3	−7
		20		
−9	−45			
		−9		
				−42

×		2	−6
		8	
	15		−45
		6	
7			63

29. Use arrows on each of the following number lines to find the value of each of the following.

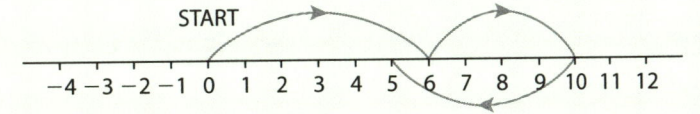

Remember: −(−4) = +4

(a) 6 + 4 − 5 =   5

(b) −3 + 8 − 4 + =

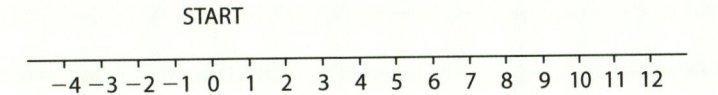

(c) 5 − (−3) + 2 =

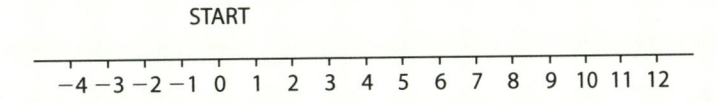

(d) −3 − 2 + 6 =

(e) 2 − 5 − (−4) =

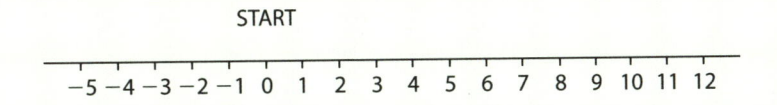

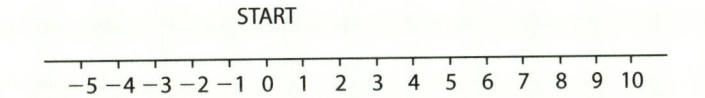

(f) 7 − 9 − (−3) =

Date ....   Signed ....

2.3 Index form… a^n, $a \in Z$

(i) $(-3) \times (-3) \times (-3) = (-3)^3$
(ii) $(-2) \times (-2) \times (-4) \times (-4) \times (-4) = (-2)^2 \times (-4)^3$

Write each of the following in index form.

1. $(-5) \times (-5) \times (-5) \times (-5) \times (-5) =$

2. $(-3) \times (-3) \times (-3) \times (-3) =$

3. $(-7) \times (-7) \times (-7) =$

4. $(-2) \times (-2) \times (-3) \times (-3) =$

5. $\dfrac{(-6) \times (-6) \times (-6)}{(-3) \times (-3)} =$

6. $(-8) \times (-8) \times (-8) \times (-8) \times (-8) \times (-8) =$

7. $\dfrac{(-2) \times (-2)}{(-3) \times (-3) \times (-3)} =$

8. $(-4) \times (-5) \times (-4) \times (-5) =$

9. $(-3) \times (-4) \times (-3) \times (-4) \times (-3) =$

10. $\dfrac{(-3) \times (-3) \times (-4) \times (-4) \times (-4)}{(-5) \times (-5)} =$

Example: Simplify (a) $(-2)^4 \times (-2)^3$ $= (-2)^7$
(b) $\dfrac{(-3)^5}{(-3)^2}$ $= (-3)^3$

Simplify each of the following.

1. $(-5)^3 \times (-2)^3 =$

2. $(-3)^5 \times (-3)^2 =$

3. $(-7)^4 \times (-7)^4 =$

4. $(-8)^6 \times -8 =$

5. $(-6)^2 \times (-6)^3 =$

6. $(-2)^3 \times (-2)^4 \times (-2)^2 =$

7. $(-5)^3 \times (-5)^4 \times (-5)^5 =$

8. $(-7)^2 \times (-7)^8 \times (-7) =$

9. $(-4)^4 \times (-4)^3 \times (-4)^2 =$

10. $(-3)^3 \times (-3) \times (-3)^4 =$

11. $\dfrac{(-4)^4}{(-4)^2} =$

12. $\dfrac{(-5)^5}{(-5)^4} =$

13. $\dfrac{(-6)^7}{-6} =$

14. $\dfrac{(-3)^4 \times (-3)^5}{(-3)^3} =$

15. $\dfrac{(-8)^5 \times (-8)^4}{(-8)^2 \times (-8)^3} =$

16. $\dfrac{(-9)^{10}}{(-9)^3 \times (-9)^5} =$

17. $\dfrac{(-7)^4 \times (-7)^8}{(-7)^3 \times (-7)^5} =$

18. $\dfrac{(-6)^3 \times (-6)^7}{(-6)^2 \times (-6)^4} =$

Date .... Signed ....

2.4 Integers: Order ≤, ≥, >, <

Example: Find the integers x that satisfy

(a) $-2 \leq x \leq 4$ $\quad$ −2, −1, 0, 1, 2, 3, 4

(b) $-4 < x < 2$ $\quad$ −3, −2, −1, 0, 1

1. Find the integers x that satisfy each of the following.

   (a) $-3 \leq x \leq 2$ $\quad\quad\quad\quad\quad\quad\quad$ (f) $-1 < x < 2$

   (b) $-5 \leq x \leq -1$ $\quad\quad\quad\quad\quad\quad$ (g) $-3 \leq x < -1$

   (c) $-4 < x \leq 0$ $\quad\quad\quad\quad\quad\quad\quad$ (h) $-5 < x < -3$

   (d) $-9 < x < -5$ $\quad\quad\quad\quad\quad\quad$ (i) $-4 < x < 0$

   (e) $-1 \leq x \leq 3$ $\quad\quad\quad\quad\quad\quad\quad$ (j) $0 \leq x \leq 3$

2.5 Rounding Integers

Example: By rounding to the nearest 10, estimate the value of

(a) $12 \times (-23)$ $\quad\quad\quad$ $10 \times (-20) = -200$

(b) $(-17) \times (-33)$ $\quad\quad$ $(-20) \times (-30) = +600$

2. By rounding to the nearest 10, estimate the value of each of the following.

   (a) $16 \times (-27) = \quad\quad =$ $\quad\quad$ (e) $19 \times (-11) = \quad\quad =$

   (b) $\dfrac{-64}{23} = \quad\quad =$ $\quad\quad$ (f) $(-16) \times (-16) = \quad\quad =$

   (c) $(-51) \times (-14) = \quad\quad =$ $\quad\quad$ (g) $\dfrac{(-44)}{(-14)} = \quad\quad =$

   (d) $26 \times (-19) = \quad\quad =$ $\quad\quad$ (h) $\dfrac{-68}{-23} = \quad\quad =$

3. (a) Find two numbers that have a sum of 4 and a difference of 10.

   (b) Find three consecutive numbers that total -12.

   (c) If $20 + x < 20$, what can you say about x?.

4. A submarine was 246 metres below sea level. It first rose 14 metres and then dived a further 80 metres. How far was it then below sea level?

Date .... $\quad\quad$ Signed ....

3.1 Rational Numbers: Decimals – Fractions – Percentages

1. Write the value of the underlined digit as a fraction.

   (a) 2.765 → $\frac{7}{10}$

   (b) 0.914 →

   (c) 12.84 →

   (d) 36.94 →

   (e) 7.21 →

   (f) 1.318 →

   (g) 15.416 →

   (h) 0.0145 →

   (i) 1.001 →

   (j) 30.01 →

   (k) 171.1 →

   (l) 4.0101 →

2. Write these numbers as decimals.

   (a) Four and seven hundredths →

   (b) Twelve and four tenths →

   (c) Fourteen and six thousandths →

   (d) Twenty six and thirty seven thousandths →

   (e) Thirty nine and one hundred and four thousandths →

   (f) Forty five and eighteen hundredths →

3. Using the scale on each number line, write down the value of each labelled point.

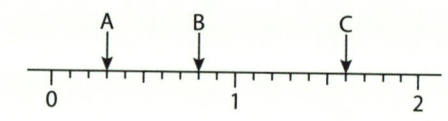

   A =   B =   C 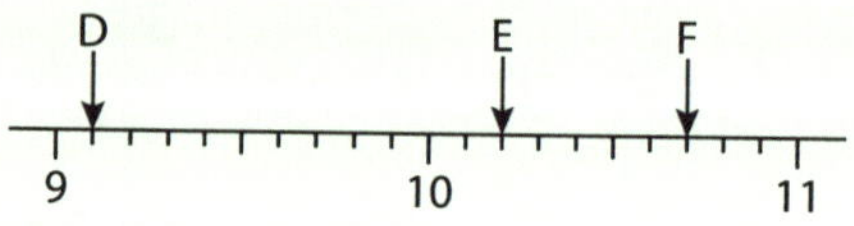 =   D =   E =   F =

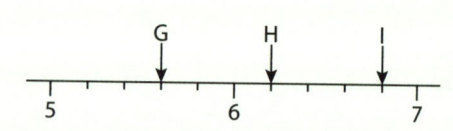

   G =   H =   I 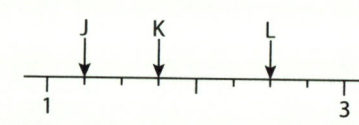 =   J =   K =   L =

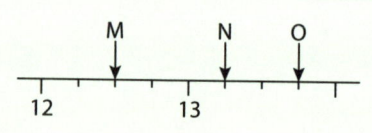

   M =   N =   O 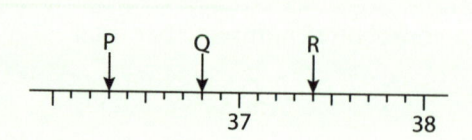 =   P =   Q =   R =

   Date ....   Signed ....

4. Write down the value of each given point on these number lines.

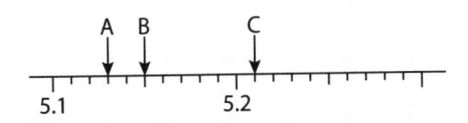

A =   B =   C 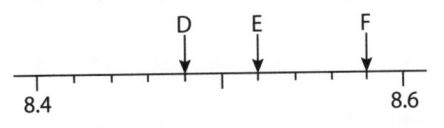 =   D =   E =   F =

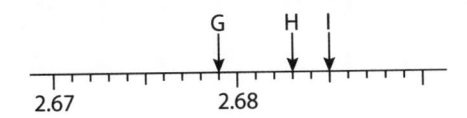

G =   H =   I 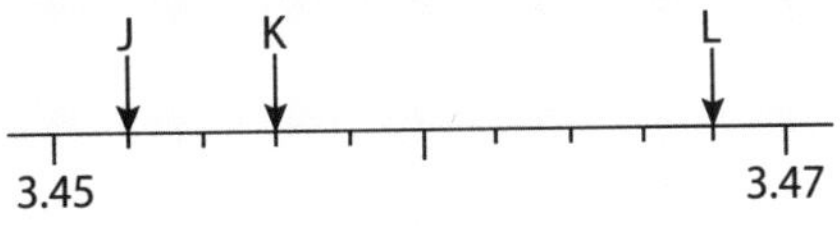 =   J =   K =   L =

5. Find the decimal that is midway between the following.

(a) 3.6 and 3.7

(b) 2.1 and 2.2

(c) 3.9 and 4

(d) 0 and 0.1

(e) 5.36 and 5.37

(f) 7.89 and 8

> Note $2.46 \times 10 = 24.6$ $2.46 \div 10 = 0.246$
> $2.46 \times 100 = 246.0$ $2.46 \div 100 = 0.0246.$

6. Complete the table.

	Number	× 10	× 100	× 1000
1.	1.17			
2.	0.43			
3.	10.03			
4.	73.1			
5.	0.0032			

	Number	÷ 10	÷ 100	÷ 1000
1.	24.12			
2.	3.07			
3.	0.04			
4.	73.2			
5.	167.1			

7. Work out each of the following.

(a) 3.69×10

(b) $2.5 \div 10$

(c) 0.31×10

(d) 0.042×10

(e) $0.04 \div 10$

(f) $573 \div 10$

(g) 10×4.03

(h) $0.76 \div 10$

(i) 10.2×10

(j) 10×0.002

(k) $0.045 \div 10$

(l) 10.05×10

Date ....   Signed ....

8. (a) 1.4 × 100

(b) 3.24 ÷ 100

(c) 40.36 ÷ 1000

(d) 0.032 × 1000

(e) 19.72 ÷ 100

(f) 19.15 × 10

(g) 176.4 ÷ 100

(h) 100.4 ÷ 1000

(i) 2.004 × 100

(j) 0.032 ÷ 100

9. Write these numbers in order starting with the smallest.

(a) 2, 2.9, 2.849, 2.85, 2.499

(b) 6.127, 6.123, 6.12, 6.129, 6.192

(c) 0.0838, 0.0829, 0.083, 0.0832

(d) 18.1, 18.09, 18.18, 18.099, 18.178

(e) 11.3, 11.56, 11.18, 11.29, 11.06

10. Complete the following table.

	Number	Correct to the nearest whole number	Correct to one place of decimals	Correct to two places of decimals
1.	6.273			
2.	4.719			
3.	12.163			
4.	0.788			
5.	7.654			
6.	10.842			
7.	127.472			
8.	0.098			
9.	15.483			
10.	7.555			

11. Find the value of each of the following.

(a) 1.6 + 2.1 =

(b) 0.5 + 1.8 =

(c) 2.3 − 1.4 =

(d) 5.9 + 4.2 =

(e) 8.7 − 6.1 =

(f) 11.2 − 8.3 =

(g) 4.82 + 0.12 =

(h) 3.17 + 1.62 =

(i) 9.42 − 3.21 =

(j) 8.88 + 2.22 =

(k) 3.48 − 2.54 =

(l) 0.23 − 0.19 =

(m) 3 × 2.3 =

(n) 1.6 × 5 =

(o) 2 × 7.3 =

(p) 4.7 × 3 =

(q) 2.1 × 6 =

(r) 0.7 × 1.2 =

Date .... Signed ....

3.2 Adding and Subtracting Fractions

By getting common denominators, write each of the following as a scale fraction.

1. $\frac{1}{2} + \frac{1}{3} =$ $\frac{3}{6} + \frac{2}{6}$ $= \frac{5}{6}$
2. $\frac{3}{4} + \frac{1}{3} =$ $=$
3. $\frac{5}{6} - \frac{1}{3} =$ $=$
4. $\frac{1}{4} + \frac{1}{5} =$ $=$
5. $\frac{4}{5} - \frac{1}{10} =$ $=$
6. $\frac{4}{9} - \frac{2}{3} =$ $=$
7. $\frac{2}{3} - \frac{2}{5} =$ $=$
8. $\frac{2}{5} + \frac{2}{3} =$ $=$
9. $\frac{1}{7} + \frac{2}{7} =$ $=$
10. $\frac{1}{3} - \frac{1}{4} =$ $=$
11. $\frac{1}{5} + \frac{1}{3} =$ $=$
12. $\frac{1}{4} - \frac{1}{5} =$ $=$
13. $\frac{1}{10} + \frac{4}{5} =$ $=$
14. $\frac{3}{7} - \frac{1}{3} =$ $=$
15. $\frac{2}{9} + \frac{1}{5} =$ $=$
16. $\frac{2}{7} + \frac{1}{4} =$ $=$
17. $\frac{3}{8} - \frac{1}{5} =$ $=$
18. $\frac{1}{3} - \frac{1}{6} =$ $=$
19. $\frac{3}{2} - \frac{1}{3} =$ $=$
20. $\frac{3}{4} - \frac{1}{3} =$ $=$
21. $\frac{3}{10} - \frac{3}{20} =$ $=$
22. $\frac{4}{30} + \frac{3}{20} =$ $=$
23. $\frac{5}{9} - \frac{3}{8} =$ $=$
24. $\frac{3}{11} - \frac{1}{4} =$ $=$
25. $\frac{1}{2} - \frac{4}{9} =$ $=$
26. $\frac{1}{3} + \frac{4}{7} =$ $=$
27. $\frac{13}{20} + \frac{3}{100} =$ $=$
28. $\frac{29}{100} + \frac{13}{50} =$ $=$
29. $\frac{6}{1000} + \frac{15}{100} =$ $=$
30. $\frac{31}{100} - \frac{4}{10} =$ $=$ ***

Express each of the following fractions in its simplest form.

1. $\frac{2}{8} =$
2. $\frac{5}{15} =$
3. $\frac{7}{21} =$
4. $\frac{12}{16} =$
5. $\frac{8}{12} =$
6. $\frac{16}{24} =$
7. $\frac{18}{30} =$
8. $\frac{8}{28} =$
9. $\frac{21}{28} =$
10. $\frac{14}{35} =$
11. $\frac{24}{72} =$
12. $\frac{22}{77} =$

Date .... Signed ....

Add each of the following.

1. $1\frac{1}{2} + 2\frac{1}{8} =$ $3\frac{4+1}{8}$ $= 3\frac{5}{8}$

2. $2\frac{3}{4} + 1\frac{1}{2} =$

3. $2\frac{1}{3} + 1\frac{1}{2} =$

4. $1\frac{3}{4} + 2\frac{3}{8} =$

5. $1\frac{3}{10} + 1\frac{4}{5} =$

6. $2\frac{3}{5} + 1\frac{2}{3} =$

7. $4\frac{1}{4} + 2\frac{5}{8} =$

8. $2\frac{5}{6} + 3\frac{1}{3} =$

9. Arrange these fractions in order, starting with the smallest.

  (a) $\frac{1}{4}, \frac{3}{8}, \frac{1}{2}, \frac{5}{8}, \frac{3}{4}, \frac{1}{8}, \frac{7}{8}.$

  (b) $\frac{1}{3}, \frac{5}{6}, \frac{1}{2}, \frac{1}{6}, \frac{2}{3}.$

  (c) $\frac{3}{10}, \frac{2}{5}, \frac{1}{2}, \frac{7}{10}, \frac{4}{5}.$

  (d) $\frac{1}{4}, \frac{1}{3}, \frac{1}{2}, \frac{1}{6}, \frac{1}{5}.$

  (e) $\frac{1}{4}, \frac{2}{3}, \frac{1}{2}, \frac{5}{6}, \frac{3}{5}.$

Subtract each of the following.

1. $2\frac{1}{2} - 1\frac{1}{4} =$ $1\frac{2-1}{4}$ $= 1\frac{1}{4}$

2. $2\frac{1}{2} - 1\frac{1}{5} =$

3. $1\frac{4}{5} - \frac{2}{5} =$

4. $3\frac{3}{4} - 1\frac{1}{2} =$

5. $3\frac{3}{4} - 2\frac{1}{8} =$

6. $3\frac{1}{2} - \frac{1}{3} =$

7. $4\frac{2}{5} - 2\frac{1}{10} =$

8. $3\frac{5}{12} - 1\frac{5}{6} =$ ***

Complete the magic squares in which each row, column and diagonal have the same value.

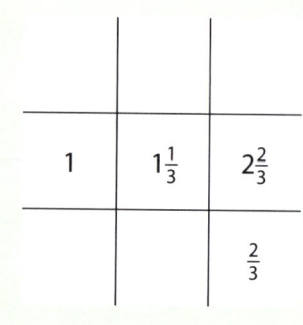

1	$1\frac{1}{3}$	$2\frac{2}{3}$
	$\frac{2}{3}$	

$1\frac{1}{8}$	$\frac{1}{4}$	$\frac{7}{8}$
		$\frac{3}{8}$

Date ....   Signed ....

3.3 Multiplying and Dividing Fractions

Multiply each of the following fractions.

1. $\frac{1}{2} \times \frac{1}{4} = \quad \frac{1}{8}$
2. $\frac{2}{3} \times \frac{1}{3} =$
3. $\frac{3}{4} \times \frac{1}{2} =$
4. $\frac{3}{8} \times \frac{1}{2} =$
5. $\frac{3}{5} \times \frac{1}{7} =$
6. $\frac{3}{4} \times \frac{2}{5} =$
7. $\frac{3}{5} \times \frac{2}{5} =$
8. $\frac{3}{7} \times \frac{5}{9} =$
9. $1\frac{1}{2} \times \frac{1}{2} = \quad \frac{3}{2} \times \frac{1}{2} = \frac{3}{4}$
10. $3\frac{1}{4} \times \frac{1}{2} =$
11. $4\frac{1}{2} \times \frac{2}{3} =$
12. $\frac{5}{6} \times 1\frac{1}{2} =$
13. $3\frac{1}{2} \times 1\frac{1}{2} =$
14. $2\frac{2}{3} \times 1\frac{1}{4} =$
15. $3\frac{2}{5} \times 2\frac{1}{3} =$

Calculate each of the following quantities.

1. $\frac{1}{4}$ of €2400 = $\quad \frac{1}{4} \times 2400 = €600$
2. $\frac{3}{4}$ of 36 hrs =
3. $\frac{2}{5}$ of €700 =
4. $\frac{2}{9}$ of 450 km =
5. $\frac{2}{5}$ of 240 min =
6. $\frac{3}{5}$ of 365 days =
7. $\frac{2}{3}$ of 42 pupils =
8. $\frac{5}{8}$ of €320 =

Divide each of the following.

1. $\frac{3}{4} \div \frac{1}{2} = \quad \frac{3}{4} \times \frac{2}{1} = \frac{6}{4} = \frac{3}{2}$
2. $\frac{2}{3} \div \frac{5}{6} =$
3. $\frac{5}{8} \div \frac{3}{4} =$
4. $\frac{2}{5} \div \frac{9}{10} =$
5. $\frac{3}{4} \div \frac{9}{14} =$
6. $\frac{4}{9} \div \frac{2}{3} =$
7. $2\frac{2}{3} \div \frac{2}{3} =$
8. $4\frac{1}{2} \div \frac{3}{4} =$
9. $1\frac{3}{8} \div \frac{3}{4} =$
10. $4\frac{1}{5} \div 3\frac{1}{2} =$

Find the total value of

1. $\frac{1}{3}$ of €24 + $\frac{1}{2}$ of €56 =
2. $\frac{1}{5}$ of €40 + $\frac{1}{6}$ of €48 =
3. $\frac{1}{4}$ of €84 − $\frac{1}{3}$ of €48 =
4. $\frac{1}{2}$ of €240 − $\frac{1}{5}$ of €85 =
5. $\frac{2}{3}$ of €36 + $\frac{1}{2}$ of €48 =
6. $\frac{1}{8}$ of €96 − $\frac{2}{3}$ of €12 =
7. $\frac{5}{6}$ of €36 − $\frac{2}{3}$ of €24 =
8. $\frac{3}{10}$ of €120 + $\frac{2}{5}$ of €45 =

Date .... Signed ....

3.4 BOMDAS and Fractions

Simplify each of the following.

1. $\left(\frac{2}{3} \div \frac{5}{6}\right) \times 2\frac{1}{4} =$ $\left(\frac{2}{\cancel{3}_1} \times \frac{\cancel{6}^2}{5}\right) \times \frac{9}{4} = \frac{1\cancel{4}}{5} \times \frac{9}{\cancel{4}_1} = \frac{9}{5}$

2. $\left(\frac{3}{4} \times \frac{2}{9}\right) \div \frac{1}{12} =$

3. $\left(\frac{2}{3} \div \frac{6}{7}\right) \times 3 =$

4. $\left(\frac{2}{5} \times \frac{1}{2}\right) \div \frac{3}{4} =$

5. $1\frac{1}{3} \times \left(\frac{3}{10} \div \frac{1}{2}\right) =$

6. $\left(3\frac{1}{3} \div 1\frac{1}{2}\right) \times \frac{9}{10} =$

7. What fraction is each arrow pointing to?

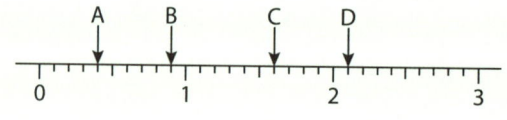

   A = $\frac{4}{10}$ B =   C =   D =

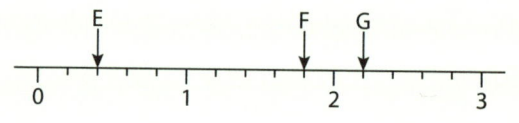

   E =   F =   G =

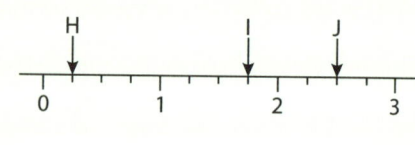

   H =   I =   J =

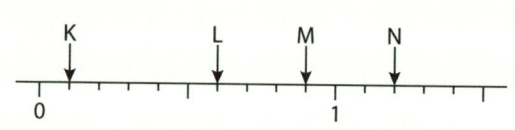

   K =   L =   M =   N =

8. This table shows information about the number of people watching a fireworks display. Complete the table.

	Men	Women	Children
Fraction of people	$\frac{3}{10}$	$\frac{1}{10}$	
Number of people		50	

9. This table shows information about the number of people watching a football match. Complete the table.

	Men	Women	Children
Fraction of people	$\frac{5}{8}$		$\frac{1}{4}$
Number of people			60

Date ....   Signed ....

3.5 Fraction Problems

1. Jim cycled $2\frac{2}{3}$ km to a village and then $3\frac{1}{4}$ km further to a friend. Find the total distance he travelled.

   Total =

2. There are 70 pupils in first year. $\frac{1}{5}$ of them come to school by bus, $\frac{3}{10}$ come by bicycle, and the rest walk.
   (a) What fraction of students walk?
   (b) How many students walk?

   (a)
   (b)

3. There are 240 animals on a farm. $\frac{5}{8}$ of then are sheep, $\frac{1}{10}$ are pigs. There are 2 horses, 4 dogs and the rest are cows. How many cows are on the farm?

   Number of sheep =
   Number of pigs =
   Number of horses =
   Number of dogs =
   Total =
   } Number of cows =

4. A garage sells $\frac{5}{9}$ of its petrol sales for the week on Saturday and Sunday. If it sells 4320 litres of petrol from Monday to Friday calculate the total number of litres sold for the whole week.

   = 4320 litres

   Number of litres (total) =

5. The petrol tank of a car holds 30 litres. At the beginning of a journey it is $\frac{4}{5}$ full. During the journey 9 litres are used. Find
   (a) How many litres of petrol are left in the car at the end of the journey.
   (b) What fraction of the tank contains petrol at the end of the journey.

   Number of litres at the beginning =
   Number of litres at end of journey =
   Fraction of petrol at end of journey =

6. If $\frac{3}{8}$ of a number is 96, find the number. What is $\frac{3}{4}$ of the number you have found?

   = 96
   Number =
   $\frac{3}{4}$ of number =

7. A container holds $10\frac{2}{3}$ litres of petrol and a tin can hold $\frac{2}{3}$ litre. How many times can the can be filled from the container?

   Number of cans =

8. Books are stacked to a height of 42 cm. If each book is $1\frac{3}{4}$ cm in thickness find how many books are in the stack.

   Number of books in stack =

Date ....   Signed ....

3.6 Percentages/Fractions

Change each of the following percentages → fractions.

1. 25% = $\frac{25}{100} = \frac{1}{4}$

2. 10% =

3. 5% =

4. 50% =

5. 75% =

6. 80% =

7. 15% =

8. $33\frac{1}{3}$% =

9. 60% =

10. 125% =

Change each of the following fractions → percentages.

11. $\frac{1}{4}$ = $\frac{1}{4} \times \frac{100}{1}\% = 25\%$

12. $\frac{1}{8}$ =

13. $\frac{1}{10}$ =

14. $\frac{1}{5}$ =

15. $\frac{2}{5}$ =

16. $\frac{3}{8}$ =

17. $\frac{2}{3}$ =

18. $\frac{7}{10}$ =

19. $\frac{7}{20}$ =

20. $\frac{13}{20}$ =

Write down the fraction of each of the following shapes which is shaded.

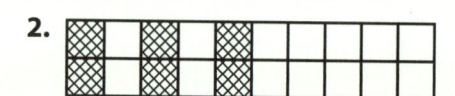

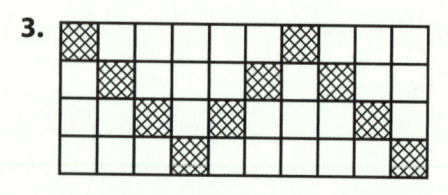

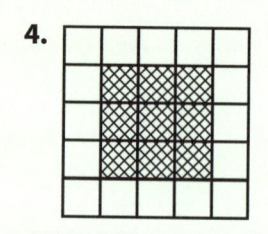

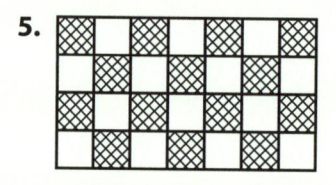

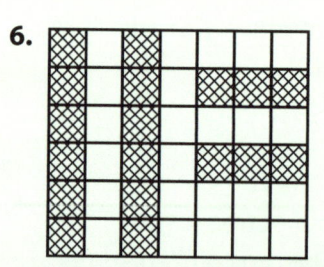

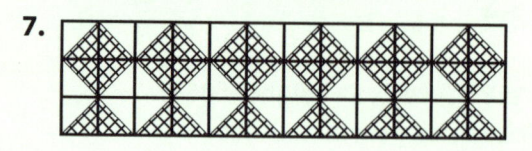

1.
2.
3.
4.
5.
6.
7.

Date ....   Signed ....

Shade in the percentage for each of the following. (Write each percentage as a fraction first.)

1. 40% = $\frac{40}{100} = \frac{2}{5}$

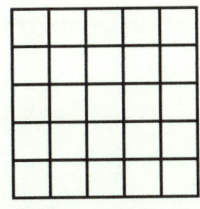

2. 75% =

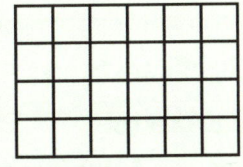

3. 16% =

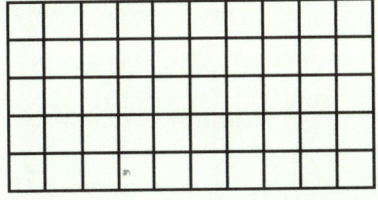

4. 28% =

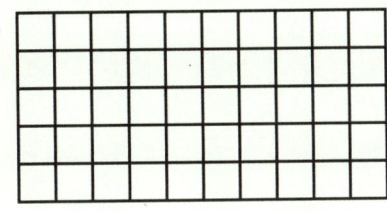

5. 25% =

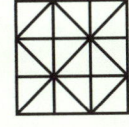

6. $12\frac{1}{2}$% =

Change the following decimals to percentages and percentages to decimals.

1. .40 = $\frac{40}{100}$ = 40%

2. .25 = $\frac{25}{100} = 25$ % ✓

3. .65 = $\frac{65}{100} = 65$% ✓

4. .36 = $\frac{36}{100} = 36$% ✓

5. 1.25 = $\frac{125}{100} = 125$% ✓

6. 0.02 = $\frac{2}{100} = 2$% ✓

7. 0.50 = $\frac{50}{100} = 50$% ✓

8. 14% = $\frac{14}{100}$ = .14

9. 8% = $\frac{8}{100} = .08$ ✓

10. 1% = $\frac{1}{100} = .01$ ✓

11. 90% = $\frac{90}{100} = .9$ ✓

12. 110% = $\frac{110}{100} = 1.1$ ✓

13. 75% = $\frac{75}{100} = .75$ ✓

14. 8.5% = $\frac{8½}{100} = .085$

15. 0.22 = $\frac{22}{100} = 22$ % ✓

16. 60% = $\frac{60}{100} = .6$ ✓

17. 0.30 = $\frac{30}{100} = 30$ % ✓

18. 250% = $\frac{250}{100} = 2.5$

19. 0.18 = $\frac{18}{100} = 18$ % ✓

20. 1.20 = $\frac{120}{100} = 1.2$ %

21. 44% = $\frac{44}{100} = .44$

Complete the table.

Fraction	Decimal	Percentage
2/5	0.4	40%
$\frac{7}{20}$	0.35	35%
19/20	0.95	95%
13/20	0.65	65%
$\frac{12}{25}$	0.48	48%

Date .... Signed ....

4.1 Significant Figures

1. Correct each of the following to the number of significant figures shown.

Number	Correct to 2 significant figures	Correct to 3 significant figures
2718	2700	2720
−40170	−40000	−40200
7865		
−3916		
25063		
−19785		
64324		
−145629		
3784711		
27.18		
2.718		
0.2718		
0.02718		

2. Each of the following numbers has been corrected to 2 significant figures. Write down (i) the largest (ii) the smallest possible values of the original numbers.

		Largest	Smallest
(a)	370		
(b)	1600		
(c)	−2300		
(d)	17		
(e)	−310		
(f)	6500		
(g)	−8900		
(h)	0.0015		

3. Calculate the error in correcting each of the following numbers to 2 significant figures.

Remember:
Error = Original number − Corrected number

		Correct to 2 sig. fig.	Error
(a)	317		
(b)	1629		
(c)	49817		
(d)	7816		
(e)	1555		

Date .... Signed ....

4.2 Using Your Calculator

Remember:
1. Use brackets where indicated.
2. Use the fraction button ▤ or a/b
3. Use the index (power) button y^x

1. Use your calculator to find the value of each of the following.
   (Use the change button to express your answer as a fraction.)

   (i) $3 + 5(8 + 3) =$

   (ii) $3 \times 4 + 2 =$

   (iii) $3 \times (4 + 2) =$

   (iv) $5 \times 4 - 6 \times 2 =$

   (v) $6 \times 8 + 8 \div 2 =$

   (vi) $(16 - 7)(18 + 3) =$

   (vii) $12(4 + 14) - 156 =$

   (viii) $8 + 6(3 + 13) =$

   (ix) $\dfrac{36 + 27}{9} =$

   (x) $\dfrac{3(15 + 12)}{2 + 16} =$

   (xi) $2^4 \times 3^2 =$

   (xii) $\sqrt{125} \times 4^3 =$

   (xiii) $\dfrac{\sqrt{147}}{\sqrt{3}} =$

   (xiv) $\dfrac{\sqrt{6(13 + 12)}}{\sqrt{5} + 1} =$

   (xv) $\dfrac{2^6 \times 3^4}{4^2} =$

   (xvi) $\dfrac{\sqrt{3(11 + 16)}}{\sqrt{4^3}} =$

   (xvii) $\dfrac{3 \times 27 + 6 \times 54}{256 - 92} =$

   (xviii) $\sqrt{169}\,(27 - 15) =$

   (xix) $\dfrac{72}{14} + \dfrac{16}{9} - \dfrac{8}{3} =$

   (xx) $\dfrac{27 \times 45}{3(46 - 11)} =$

2. Use your calculator to find the value of each of the following, correct to 2 places of decimals.

   (i) $\dfrac{274 \times 196}{4^3 \times 3^3} =$

   (ii) $\dfrac{\dfrac{39}{14} + \dfrac{64}{3}}{\sqrt{109}} =$

   (iii) $\dfrac{74 \times (27 + 69)}{\sqrt{19 + 69}} =$

   (iv) $\dfrac{3(16 + 27)}{\sqrt{50} - \sqrt{30}} =$

   (v) $(19 + \sqrt{3})(\sqrt{14} - 2) =$

   (vi) $\dfrac{8\sqrt{23}}{4\sqrt{19}} =$

   (vii) $\dfrac{37(9 + \sqrt{28})}{16 + 29\sqrt{13}} =$

   (viii) $\dfrac{176 \times 739}{\sqrt{196} + 47} =$

Date .... Signed ....

4.3 Number Lines

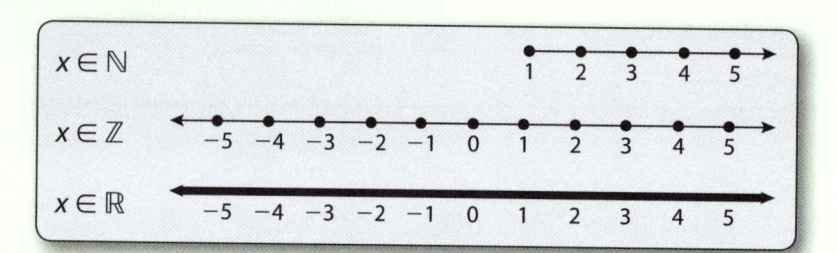

$x \in \mathbb{N}$ 1 2 3 4 5	< less than
$x \in \mathbb{Z}$ −5 −4 −3 −2 −1 0 1 2 3 4 5	⩽ less than or equal to
$x \in \mathbb{R}$ −5 −4 −3 −2 −1 0 1 2 3 4 5	> greater than
	⩾ greater than or equal to

Using each of the number lines provided, plot the following sets of points.

1. $x \leq 4$ and $x \in \mathbb{N}$

2. $x < 3$ and $x \in \mathbb{N}$

3. $x \geq 2$ and $x \in \mathbb{N}$

4. $x \geq 3$ and $x \in \mathbb{N}$

5. $x \geq -4$ and $x \in \mathbb{Z}$

6. $x < 2$ and $x \in \mathbb{Z}$

7. $x > 4$ and $x \in \mathbb{Z}$

8. $x \leq -2$ and $x \in \mathbb{Z}$

9. $x \geq -2$ and $x \in \mathbb{Z}$

10. $x < 4$ and $x \in \mathbb{Z}$

11. $x < 5$ and $x \in \mathbb{N}$

12. $x < 4$ and $x \in \mathbb{R}$

13. $x \geq -4$ and $x \in \mathbb{R}$

14. $x \leq 2$ and $x \in \mathbb{R}$

Date ....   Signed ....

15. $x > -3$ and $x \in \mathbb{R}$

16. $x > 2$ and $x \in \mathbb{R}$

17. $x \leq 4$ and $x \in \mathbb{R}$

18. $3 \leq x \leq 5$ and $x \in \mathbb{N}$

19. $1 \leq x < 4$ and $x \in \mathbb{N}$

20. $-2 < x \leq 5$ and $x \in \mathbb{N}$

21. $-2 \leq x < 3$ and $x \in \mathbb{Z}$

22. $-4 < x < 5$ and $x \in \mathbb{Z}$

23. $-2 < x \leq 1$ and $x \in \mathbb{Z}$

24. $1 < x < 4$ and $x \in \mathbb{R}$

25. $0 < x \leq 5$ and $x \in \mathbb{R}$

26. $-4 \leq x \leq 0$ and $x \in \mathbb{R}$

27. $-2 < x \leq 4$ and $x \in \mathbb{Z}$

28. $-3 \leq x \leq 5$ and $x \in \mathbb{Z}$

29. $1 < x < 5$ and $x \in \mathbb{R}$

30. $-1 < x < 4$ and $x \in \mathbb{R}$

31. $-5 \leq x \leq 1$ and $x \in \mathbb{R}$

Date .... Signed ....

4.4 Commutative

1. Write TRUE or FALSE after each of the following.

   (a) $4 + 5 = 5 + 4$ TRUE/FALSE

   (b) $9 + 3 = 3 + 9$ TRUE/FALSE

   (b) $3 \times 7 = 7 \times 3$

   (d) $4 - 3 = 3 - 4$

   (e) $10 \div 5 = 5 \div 10$

   (f) $6 - 9 = 9 - 6$

   (g) $8 \times 2 = 2 \times 8$

   (h) $8 \div 2 = 2 \div 8$

2. If $a, b \in \mathbb{N}$ state if each of the following are TRUE or FALSE.

   (a) $a + b = b + a$ TRUE/FALSE

   (b) $a \times b = b \times a$ TRUE/FALSE

   (b) $a - b = b - a$

   (d) $a \div b = b \div a$

4.5 Associative

1. By finding a value for each side of the equation, state if each of the following is TRUE or FALSE.

   (a) $(3 + 5) + 6 = 3 + (5 + 6)$

   (b) $(4 \times 2) \times 7 = 4 \times (2 \times 7)$

   TRUE/FALSE   TRUE/FALSE

   (c) $(8 - 5) - 3 = 8 - (5 - 3)$

   (d) $(12 \div 6) \div 2 = 12 \div (6 \div 2)$

   (e) $(6 + 1) + 8 = 6 + (1 + 8)$

   (f) $(2 - 5) - 3 = 2 - (5 - 3)$

   (g) $(3 \times 4) \times 5 = 3 \times (4 \times 5)$

   (h) $(2 \div 10) \div 5 = 2 \div (10 \div 5)$

2. If a, b and $c \in \mathbb{N}$ state if each of the following are TRUE or FALSE.

   (a) $(a + b) + c = a + (b + c)$

   (b) $(a \times b) \times c = a \times (b \times c)$

   TRUE/FALSE   TRUE/FALSE

   (c) $(a - b) - c = a - (b - c)$

   (d) $(a \div b) \div c = a \div (b \div c)$

Date ....   Signed ....

4.6 Distributive Property

$6(4+3) = 6 \times 4 + 6 \times 3$

Fill in the missing number in each of the following.

1. $3(6+4) = 3 \times 6 + 3 \times \underline{}$
2. $4(3+8) = 4 \times 3 + \underline{} \times 8$
3. $6(5+2) = 6 \times \underline{} + 6 \times 2$
4. $7(5+9) = \underline{} \times 5 + 7 \times 9$
5. $8(3+\underline{}) = 8 \times 3 + 8 \times 6$
6. $2(\underline{} + 5) = 2 \times 8 + \underline{} \times 5$
7. $\underline{}(4+5) = 6 \times 4 + 6 \times 5$
8. $3(6 + \underline{}) = 3 \times \underline{} + \underline{} \times 4$
9. $\underline{}(3 + \underline{}) = \underline{} \times \underline{} + 5 \times 7$
10. $\underline{}(\underline{} + \underline{}) = 3 \times 4 + 3 \times 5$

Order of operations: Brackets – multiplication – division – addition – subtraction.

Without using a calculator, evaluate each of the following.

1. $(4+5) \times 3 - 2 =$
2. $3 \times 2 \times (5-2) =$
3. $2 \times (3-5) + 6 =$
4. $3 \times (6-2) \times 4 =$
5. $2 - 4 \times (5-4) =$
6. $3 + 2 \times (4-5) =$
7. $4 - 5 \times (3-6) =$
8. $2 \times (3-5) + 6 =$
9. $2(4+5) - 3(7-1) =$
10. $3(7-4) + 2 \times 5 =$
11. $3(4+2) - 2(5-2) =$
12. $(8 \times 3)(5-2) =$
13. $\dfrac{3(2+4)}{2(7-4)} =$
14. $8 - 6 \div 3 =$
15. $16 \div 8 \times 2 =$
16. $16 + 8 \times 2 =$
17. $16 - 8 \div 2 =$
18. $6(3+4) - 2 =$
19. $3(6 \div 3 + 2) =$
20. $(10-6)(10 \div 2) =$
21. $4 - 6 \times 8 \div 12 =$
22. $4 + 4(8-4) =$

Date .... Signed ....

37

4.7 BOMDAS (Revision) II

Evaluate each of the following **without** using a calculator.

Remember:
$6^2 = 6.6 = 36$
$\sqrt{25} = 5$

1. $3^2 + 2 \times 5 =$
2. $5 \times 2 + 6 =$
3. $8(5 - 3) \times \sqrt{4} =$
4. $7 + 6 \div 2 =$
5. $8 \div 2 + 12 \div 3 =$
6. $3 \times 4 \times 5 =$
7. $54 \div 6 \div 3 =$
8. $19 - (9 - 5) =$
9. $\sqrt{25} - \sqrt{9} =$
10. $6^2 + 2^2 =$
11. $4 + 70 \div 5 =$
12. $10 + (8 - 4) =$
13. $10 + 8 - 4 =$
14. $30 - 22 + 6 =$
15. $30 - 22 \times 2 =$
16. $30 \div (10 \div 2) =$
17. $(45 \times 2) \div (25 - 16) =$
18. $6 - (-2) =$
19. $4 \times (8 - 2) =$
20. $4 \times 8 - 2 =$
21. $3 \times 10 + 10 \div 2 =$
22. $20 - 3 \times 6 =$
23. $5^2 - 3^2 + 2^2 =$
24. $(30 - 22) \times 2 =$
25. $10 + 8 - 4^2 =$
26. $9^2 + \sqrt{36} - 80 =$
27. $19 - 9 - 5 =$
28. $30 \div 10 \div 2 =$
29. $3 \times 2 + 10 \div 2 =$
30. $3 + 9 \times 7 - 4 =$
31. $3(10 + 10) \div 2 =$
32. $\sqrt{49} \times \sqrt{4} - 3^2 =$
33. $\sqrt{5^2 \times 2^2} =$
34. $(10 - 5)(10 + 5) =$

Date .... Signed ....

4.8 Order of Operations III

Find a value for each of the following **without** using a calculator.

1. 18 × 2 ÷ 4 =
2. 40 ÷ 4 × 7 =
2. 27 − 11 + 30 =
4. 2 × 2 × 2 × 3 =
5. 81 ÷ 3 ÷ 3 ÷ 3 =
6. 4 × 10 × 10 =

Without using a calculator, find each of the follwing missing numbers.

1. ___ × 3 × 4 = 24
2. ___ ÷ 2 ÷ 5 = 3
3. ___ × 100 ÷ 20 = 35
4. 48 ÷ ___ × 2 = 16
5. 418 − ___ − 99 = 318
6. 1000 ÷ ___ ÷ 5 = 8

Use one of the operations ×, ÷, +, − to make each calculation correct.

1. 5 ___ 7 × 2 = 19
2. 21 ___ 3 + 11 = 18
3. 18 + 6 ___ 2 = 21
4. 16 ___ 5 − 12 = 9
5. 22 − 7 ___ 3 = 12
6. 28 ___ 7 + 2 = 6
7. 21 − 5 ___ 4 = 1
8. 24 ___ 8 ___ 5 = 15
9. 12 ___ 2 ___ 4 × 5 = 26
10. 45 ___ 15 ___ 2 − 11 = 4

Complete the following table for the results of an archery contest if five people were in the final.
They each had 6 shots.
Only one bullseye was scored.
The scores are in order of size.

							TOTAL
Rajit	19	19	39	39	45	45	206
Peter		39	39		45		186
John		19		39	45		186
Helen	19			45			232
Carlo	19		39	39			200

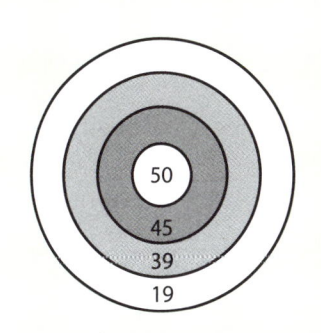

Date .... Signed ....

5.1 Element of ∈, Not an Element of ∉

Example: (a) If A = {2, 3, 4, 5, 6, 7} then 4 ∈ A, 8 ∉ A

(b) If B = {1, 2, 5, 8, a, c, e} then 4 ∉ B, e ∈ B

Insert the symbols ∈ or ∉ in each of the following.

1. If A = {2, 3, 4, 5, 6, 7} then 4 ∈ A , 6 ∈ A , 1 ∉ A , 5 ∈ A

2. If B = {1, 2, 3, 4, 5, 6, 7, 8} then 3 ∈ B , 6 ∈ B , 11 ∉ B , 9 ∉ B

3. If C = {a, b, c, d, e, f} then g ∉ C , h ∉ C , f ∈ C , b ∈ C

4. If D = {a, b, c, d, 1, 3, 4, 6, 7} then 4 ∈ D , e ∉ D , 5 ∉ D , 2 ∉ D

5. If E = {0, 3, 6, 9, c, d, e, f} then 5 ∉ E , b ∉ E , 9 ∈ E , 0 ∈ E

6. If F = {a, b, c, d, e, f, r, s, t} then p ∉ F , g ∉ F , t ∈ F , h ∉ F

7. If G = {2, 9, 4, c, 6, e, 7, g} then c ∈ G , 8 ∉ G , e ∈ G , 5 ∉ G

5.2 Listing the elements in a set

Example: List the elements in each of the following sets:

(a) The set of letters in the word Tipperary A = {T, I, P, E, R, A, Y}

(b) The even numbers between 4 and 14 B = {6, 8, 10, 12}

List the elements in each of the following sets:

1. The vowels in the word miscellaneous. A = { i, e, a, o, u }

2. The odd numbers between 2 and 13. B = { 3, 5, 7, 9, 11 }

3. The days of the week beginning with T. C = { Tuesday, Thursday }

4. Multiples of 3 greater than 5 but less than 13. D = { 6, 9, 12 }

5. The suits in a deck of cards. E = { hearts, diamonds, clubs, spades }

6. Whole numbers between 5 and 10 inclusive. F = { 5, 6, 7, 8, 9, 10 }

7. The consonants in the word MATHEMATICS. G = { M, T, H, C, S }

8. The months of the year with less than 5 letters. H = { June, April, May, July }

Date 5/9/16 Signed ....

5.3 Sets defined by a rule

Example: List the elements in each of the following sets:
A = {x/x is a day of the week beginning with the letter S}
A = {Saturday, Sunday}

A = {x/x is a number between 7 and 13}
B = {8, 9, 10, 11, 12}

List the elements in each of the following sets:

1. A = {x/x is a vowel in the word DELICIOUS}   A = { e, i, o, u, }

2. B = {x/x is a letter in the word PARALLEL}   B = { p, a, r, l, e, }

3. C = {x/x is a letter in the word KILKENNY}   C = { k, i, l, e, n, y, }

4. D = {x/x is a student in my class with a first name beginning with the letter P?}   D = { }

5. E = {x/x is a whole number between 3 and 10 inclusive}   E = { 3, 4, 5, 6, 7, 8, 9, 10, }

6. F = {x/x is a multiple of 4 between 0 and 14}   F = { 4, 8, 12, }

7. G = {x/x is a whole number between 3 and 10}   G = { 4, 5, 6, 7, 8, 9, }

8. H = {x/x is an even number between 101 and 113}   H = { 102, 104, 106, 108, 110, 112, }

9. I = {x/x is an odd number between 14 and 26}   I = { 15, 17, 19, 21, 23, 25 }

10. J = {x/x is a multiple of 5 between 0 and 30}   J = { 5, 10, 15, 20, 25, }

11. K = {x/x is a divisor of 10}   K = { 1, 2, 5, 10, }

12. L = {x/x is a divisor of 24 and a multiple of 6}   L = { 6, 12, 24, }

13. M = {x/x is a divisor of 20 and a multiple of 5}   M = { 5, 10, 20 }

14. N = {x/x is a multiple of 2 and 3 and less than 25}   N = { 22, }

15. O = {x/x is a multiple of 3 and 5 and less than 35}   O = { 30, }

Date 6/9/16   Signed

5.4 Subset/Not a Subset: ⊂/⊄

Example: (a) If A = {2, 3, 4, 5, 6, 7} then (4, 5, 6, 7) ⊂ A

(b) If B = {1, 2, 3, 4, a, c, e, f} then (3, 4, a, b) ⊄ B

Insert the symbols ⊂ or ⊄ in each of the following.

1. If A = {1, 2, 3, 4, 5, 6, 7, 10} then {1, 4, 5, 6} ⊂ A , {6, 7} ⊂ A

2. If B = {1, a, 3, c, 5, e, 7, f, 8} then {a, 3, f} ⊂ B , {1, 8, 9} ⊄ B

3. If C = {a, b, c, d, 1, 2, 3, 7, 9, 10} then {b, 3, 6, 7} ⊄ C , {b, c, d, 8} ⊄ C

4. If D = {10, a, 8, c, 6, e, 4, g, 2} then {a, e, g} ⊂ D , {g, e, c, 10} ⊂ D

5. If E = {0, a, 3, d, 5, c, 7, b, 12} then {a, d, e} ⊄ E , {d, 7, b, 12} ⊂ E

6. If F = {2, 4, 6, 8, 10, 12} then {4, 6, 12} ⊂ F , {9, 10, 11, 12} ⊄ A

7. If G = {0, a, 3, b, 5, c, 7, d, 9} then {a, 5, e} ⊄ G , {d, 9, b} ⊂ G

8. If H = {0, 1, 2, 3, 4, 5, c, 7, d, 9} then {d, 5, 0} ⊂ H , {1, 4, 5, 7, b} ⊄ H

5.5 Equality of sets

Remember: Two sets are equal if they have the same elements.

Example: Which of the following sets are equal?

A = {1, 3, a, 5, e}, B = {5, 1, 3, a, b}, C = {1, 3, 9, 5}
D = {5, 3, a, 1, e}, E = {a, 3, 5, 2}, F = {a, b, 1, 3, 5}

A = D and B = F

1. Which four pairs of the following sets are equal?

A = {2, 3, 5, 1},   B = {a, b, f, g},   C = {2, 4, 5, 1}
D = {a, e, g, h},   E = {4, 3, 1},   F = {f, g, a, b}
G = {2, 4, 1},   H = {1, 4, 3},   I = {a, g, h, e}
J = {1, 2, 5, 4},   K = {a, b, f, 3},   L = {3, a, h, f}

B = F
C = J
D = I
E = H

2. Which of the following sets are equal?

A = {a, b, c, d},   B = {d, c, b, i},   C = {c, b, i, e}
D = {i, b, c, a},   E = {b, c, i, d},   F = {i, e, f}
G = {c, b, a, e},   H = {d, i, a, e},   I = {i, e, a, b}
J = {f, i, d},   K = {d, i, f},   L = {b, a, i, e}

B = E
J = K
I = L

Date 7/9/16   Signed

5.6 Union and Intersection of Sets

Example: If A = {1, 2, 3, 4} and B = {3, 4, 5, 6}

then A∪B = {1, 2, 3, 4, 5, 6} and A∩B = {3, 4}

1. If A = {2, 3, 4, 5, 6} and B = {5, 6, 7}

then A ∪ B = { 2, 3, 4, 5, 6, 7 } and A ∩ B = { 5, 6 }

2. If C = {4, 7, 9} and D = {4, 5}

then C ∪ D = { 4, 5, 7, 9 } and C ∩ D = { 4 }

3. If E = {2, 3, 4, 5, 6, 7, 8} and F = {5, 6}

then E ∪ F = { 2, 3, 4, 5, 6, 7, 8 } and E ∩ F = { 5, 6 }

4. If G = {2, 4, 6, 8, 10, 12} and H = {3, 7, 8, 9, 10}

then G ∪ H = { 2, 3, 4, 6, 7, 8, 9, 10, 12 } and G ∩ H = { 8, 10 }

5. If I = {a, b, c, d, e} and J = {d, e, f}

then I ∪ J = { a, b, c, d, e, f } and I ∩ J = { d, e }

6. If K = {1, a, 2, b, 4, 5} and L = {b, e, 6}

then K ∪ L = { 1, a, 2, b, 4, 5, e, 6 } and K ∩ L = { b }

7. If M = {9, 3, x, y, 5, z, 9} and N = {5, 7, e, x, y}

then M ∪ N = { 9, 3, x, y, 5, z, 7, e } and M ∩ N = { x, y, 5 }

8. If O = {a, m, 3, 5, n} and P = {b, c, 2}

then O ∪ P = { a, m, 3, 5, n, b, c, 2 } and O ∩ P = { }

9. If R = {2, 4, 6, 8} and T = {3, 5, 7}

then R ∪ T = { 2, 3, 4, 5, 6, 7, 8 } and R ∩ T = { }

10. If W = {a, b, c, d, e, f} and V = {b, c, d}

then W ∪ V = { a, b, c, d, e, f } and W ∩ V = { b, c, d }

11. If X = {a, k, 3, 4} and Y = {b, c, 4, m, n}

then X ∪ Y = { a, k, 3, 4, b, c, m, n } and X ∩ Y = { 4 }

Date .... Signed ....

5.7 Universal Set – Complement of a Set

Example: If U = {1, 2, 3, 4, 5, 6, 7, 8, 9} and A = {2, 4, 6, 8} then A' = {1, 3, 5, 7, 9}

1. Given U = {1, 2, 3, 4, 5, 6, 7, 8, 9}

   If A = {1, 2, 3, 4, 5, 6}   find   A'   = { , , }
   If B = {4, 6, 8}   find   B'   = { , , , , }
   Find   (A ∪ B)   = { , , , , , }   and   (A ∪ B)' = { , }
   Find   (A ∩ B)   = { , }   and   (A ∩ B)' = { , , , , , }

2. Given U = {a, b, c, e, i, o, s, t}

   If A = {a, b, e, s}   find   A'   = { , , , }
   If B = {e, i, s, t}   find   B'   = { , , , }
   Find   (A ∪ B)   = { , , , , }   and   (A ∪ B)' = { , }
   Find   (A ∩ B)   = { , }   and   (A ∩ B)' = { , , , , }

3. Given U = {a, e, i, o, u, 2, 4, 6, 8}

   If C = {2, 4, e, i, o}   find   C'   = { , , , }
   If D = {2, 8, u, i, a}   find   D'   = { , , , }
   Find   (C ∪ D)   = { , , , , , }   and   (C ∪ D)' = { }
   Find   (C ∩ D)   = { , }   and   (C ∩ D)' = { , , , , , }

4. Given U = {1, 2, 3, 4, 5, 6, 7, 8}

   If E = {2, 3, 4, 5}   find   E'   = {
   If F = {1, 6, 7, 8}   find   F'   = {
   Find   (E ∪ F)   = {   and   (E ∪ F)' = {
   Find   (E ∩ F)   = {   and   (E ∩ F)' = {

5. Given U = {1, 2, 3, 4, 5, 6, 7, 8}

   If E = {1, 2, 3, 4, 5, 6}   find   E'   = {
   If F = {1, 6, 7, 8}   find   F'   = {
   Find   (E ∪ F)   = {   and   (E ∪ F)' = {
   Find   (E ∩ F)   = {   and   (E ∩ F)' = {

Date ....   Signed ....

5.8 Venn Diagrams I

Example: Using the following sets, complete the Venn diagram shown.

where $U = \{1, 2, 3, 4, 5, 6\}$
and $A = \{1, 3, 4\}$
$B = \{2, 4, 5\}$

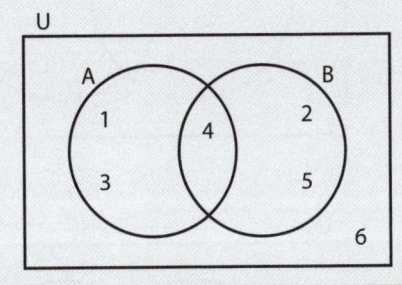

Complete the Venn diagrams shown below:

1. $U = \{1, 2, 3, 4, 5, 6, 7, 8\}$

   $C = \{2, 3, 4, 5\}$

   $D = \{1, 5, 6, 7\}$

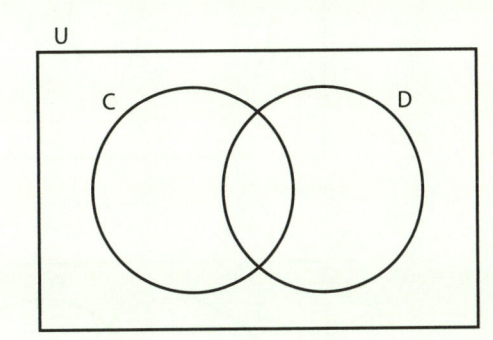

2. $U = \{2, 4, 6, 8, 10, 12, 14\}$

   $E = \{2, 4, 10, 14\}$

   $F = \{6, 8, 14\}$

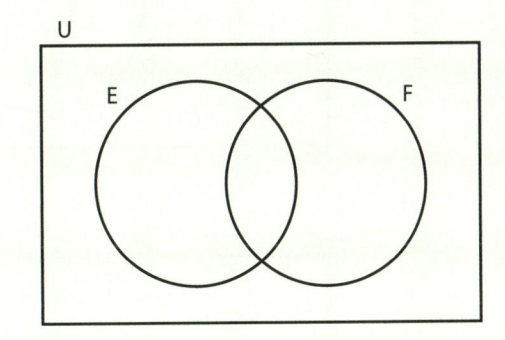

3. $U = \{a, b, c, d, e, f, g\}$

   $G = \{a, d, e\}$

   $H = \{a, b, c, d, e, f\}$

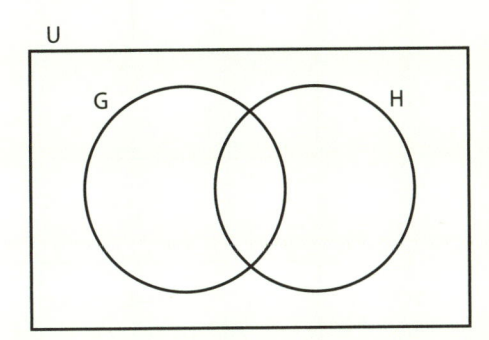

Date .... Signed ....

4. U = {1, 2, 3, 4, 5, 6}

A = {2, 3, 4, 5}

B = {2, 4, 6}

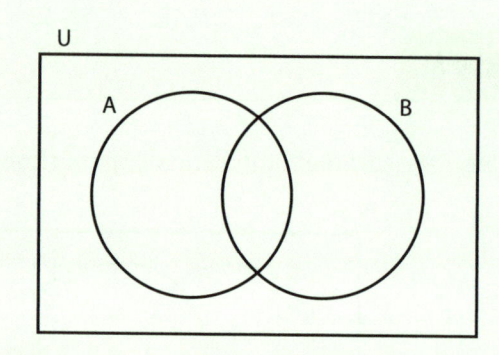

5. U = {1, 2, 3, 4, 5, 6, 7, 8}

C = {4, 5}

D = {1, 5, 8}

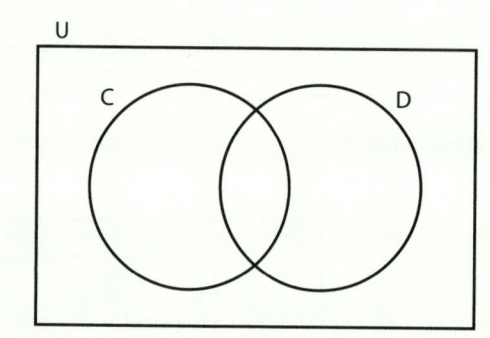

6. U = {2, 4, 6, 8, 10, 12, 14}

E = {2, 4, 10}

F = {6, 8, 14}

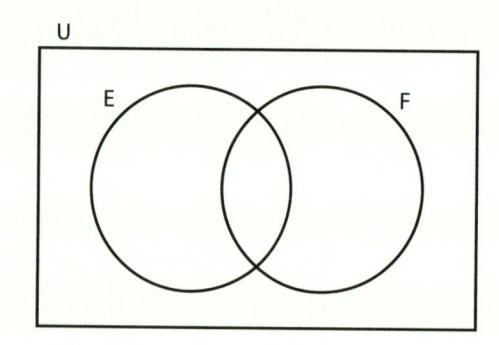

7. U = {a, b, c, d, e, f, g}

G = {a, d, e, g}

H = {a, b, c, d, e, f}

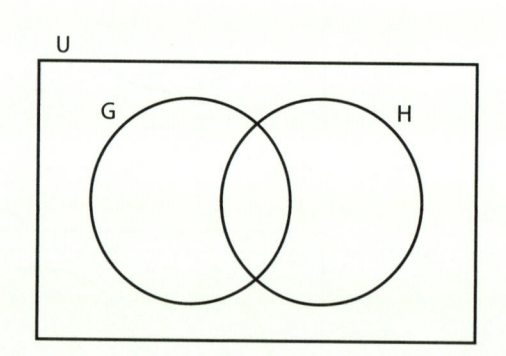

8. U = {a, b, c, d, e, f, g}

I = {d, e, g}

J = {c, d, e, g}

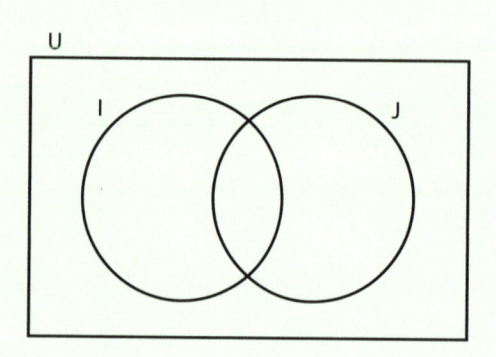

Date .... Signed ....

5.9 Venn Diagrams II

Example: Using the Venn diagrams, list the elements in each of the following sets:

U = {a, b, c, d, e, f, g, h}
K = {d, g, h}
L = {b, c, e, f, g}

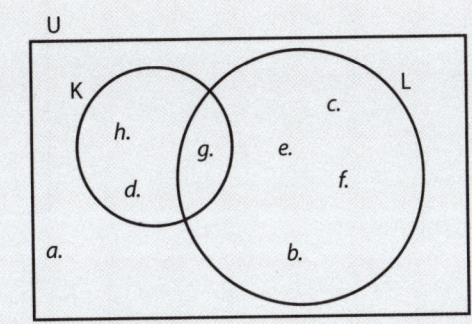

List the elements of each of the following sets:

1. U = { , , , , , , }
M = { , , }
N = { , , , }

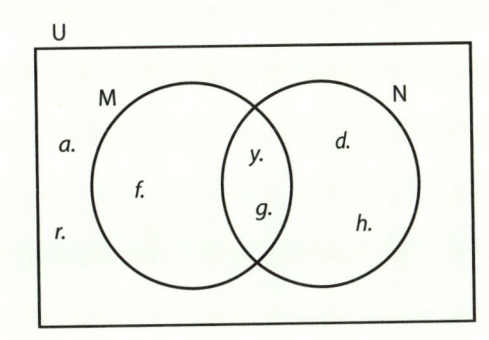

2. U = { , , , , , , , }
Q = { , , , }
P = { , , , , }

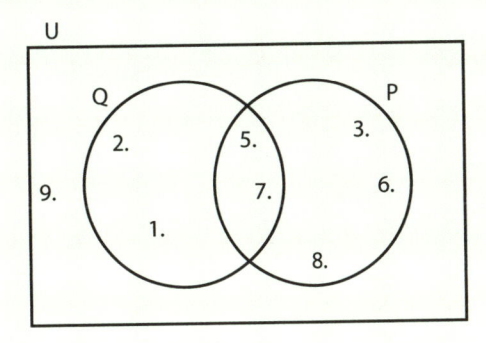

3. U = { , , , , , , , , }
S = {
T = {

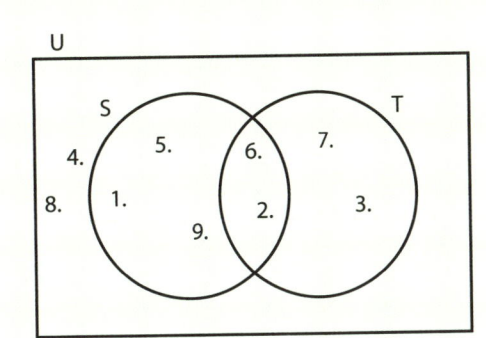

Date .... Signed ....

Using the Venn diagrams, list the elements in each of the following sets:

4. U = { , , , , , , , }

K = {

L = {

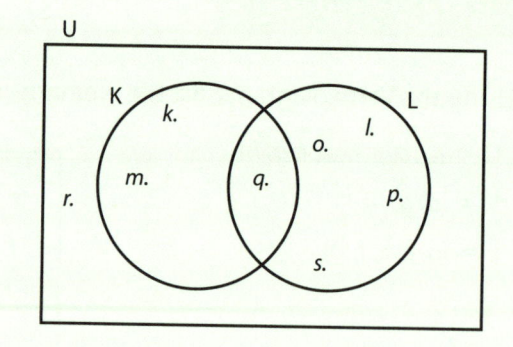

Venn diagram: U contains K and L overlapping circles. K only: k., m. Outside both (in r.): r. Intersection: q. L only: l., o., p., s.

5. U = { , , , , , }

M = {

N = {

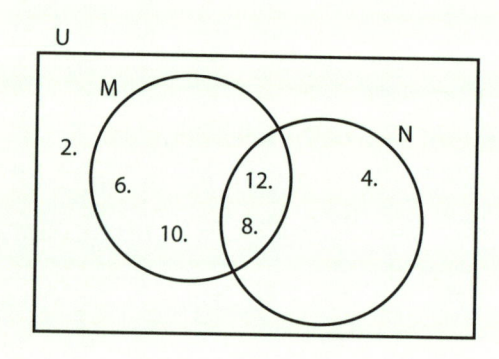

Venn diagram: U contains M and N overlapping. M only: 2., 6., 10. Intersection: 12., 8. N only: 4.

6. U = { , , , , , , }

Q = {

P = {

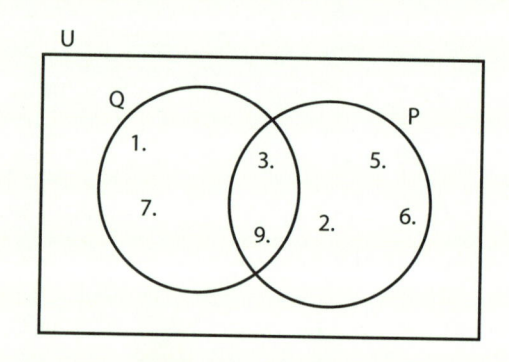

Venn diagram: U contains Q and P overlapping. Q only: 1., 7. Intersection: 3., 9. P only: 5., 2., 6.

7. U = { , , , , , , , }

S = {

T = {

Venn diagram: U contains S and T overlapping. S only: d., i., g. Outside both: a. Intersection: b., e. T only: c., h., f.

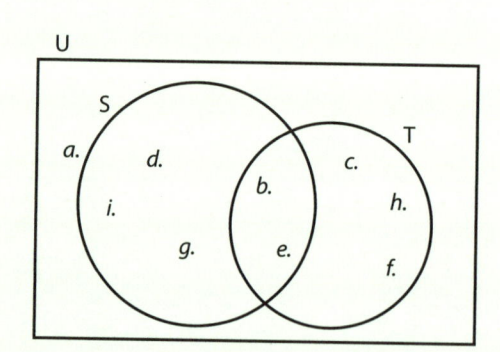

Date .... Signed ....

5.10 Venn Diagrams III

Example: Using the Venn diagrams shown, list the elements in the following sets:

U = {a, b, c, d, e, f, g, h}
K = {d, h, g}
K' = {a, b, c, e, f}
L = {c, e, f, g}
L' = {a, b, d, h}
K ∪ L = {c, d, e, f, g, h}
K ∩ L = {g}
(K ∪ L)' = {a, b}
(K ∩ L)' = {a, b, c, d, e, f, h}

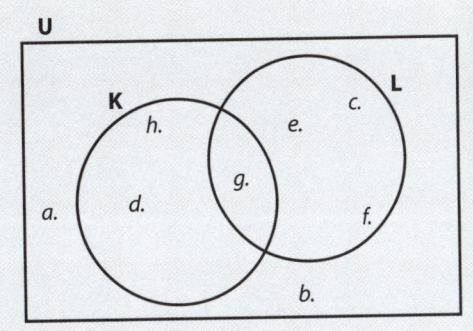

Using the Venn diagrams, list the elements in each of the following sets:

1. U = {4, 9, 1, 2, 5, 7, 3, 6, 8}
   Q = {2, 1, 5, 7}
   Q' = {4, 9, 3, 6, 8}
   P = {3, 6, 8, 5, 7}
   P' = {4, 9, 2, 1}
   Q ∪ P = {2, 1, 5, 7, 3, 6, 8}
   Q ∩ P = {5, 7}
   (Q ∪ P)' = {4, 9}
   (Q ∩ P)' = {4, 9, 2, 1, 3, 6, 8}

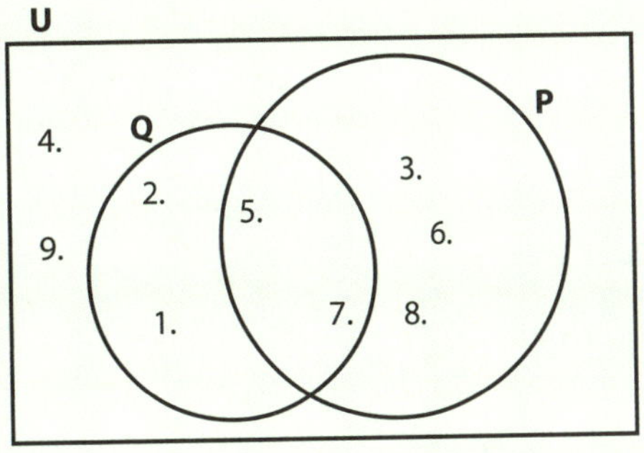

2. U = {e, 1, 9, 8, 7, d, 5}
   J = {9, 8, 7, d}
   K = {5, 8, 7, d}
   J ∪ K = {9, 8, 7, d, 5}
   (J ∪ K)' = {e, 1}
   J ∩ K = {8, 7, d}
   (J ∩ K)' = {e, 1, 9, 5}

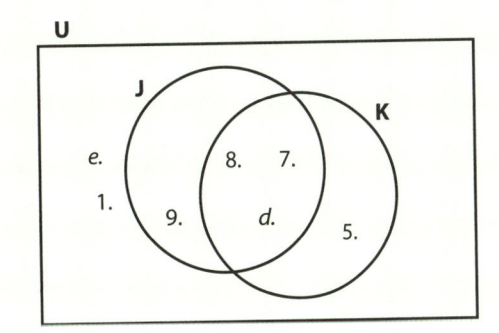

Date 12/9/16   Signed

Using the Venn diagrams, list the elements in each of the following sets:

3.
- U = { , , , , , , , , }
- S = { , , , , , }
- S' = { , , }
- R = { , , , , }
- R' = { , , , }
- R ∩ S = { , , }
- R ∪ S = { , , , , , , }
- (R ∪ S)' = { }
- (R ∩ S)' = { , , , , , }

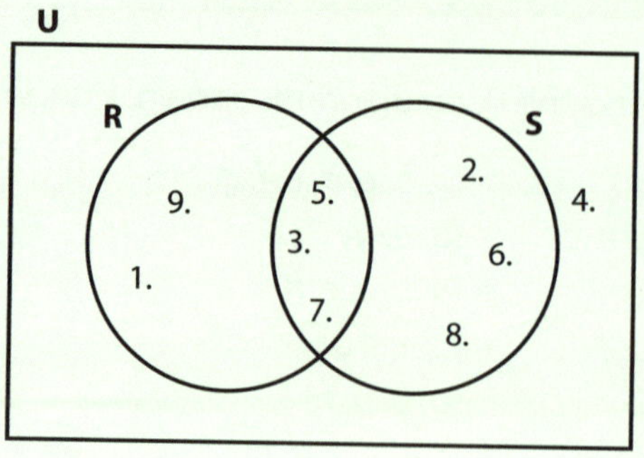

Venn diagram: U contains two overlapping circles R and S. R contains 9, 1. Intersection contains 5, 3, 7. S contains 2, 6, 8. Outside: 4.

4.
- U = {r, e, a, f, y, s, g, d, h}
- I = {a, f, y, s, g}
- I' = {d, h, r, e}
- J = {d, h, y, s, g}
- J' = {a, f, r, e}
- I ∩ J = {y, s, g}
- I ∪ J = {a, f, y, s, g, d, h}
- (I ∪ J)' = {r, e}
- (I ∩ J)' = {a, f, r, e, d, h}

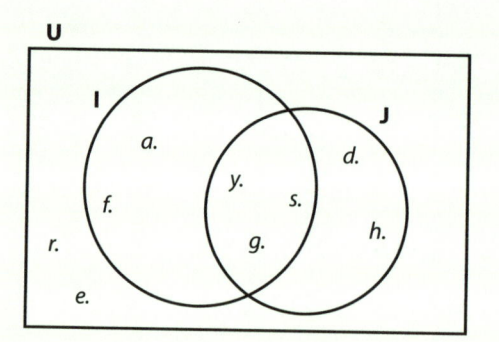

Venn diagram: U with circles I and J. I contains a, f. Intersection contains y, s, g. J contains d, h. Outside: r, e.

5.
- U = {
- A = {
- B = {
- A ∪ B = {
- (A ∪ B)' = {
- A ∩ B = {
- (A ∩ B)' = {

Venn diagram: U with circles A and B. A contains e, a. Intersection contains g, b, d. B contains c, f.

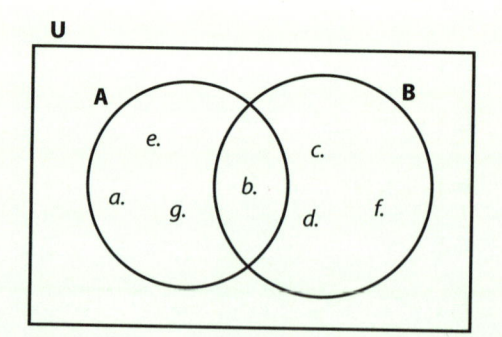

Date 12/9/16   Signed

5.11 Cardinal Number (#)

Using the Venn diagrams shown, find the cardinal number (#) of each of the following sets i.e. the number of elements in each of the sets:

Remember: If A = {a, b, c, d}, then # A = 4

1. 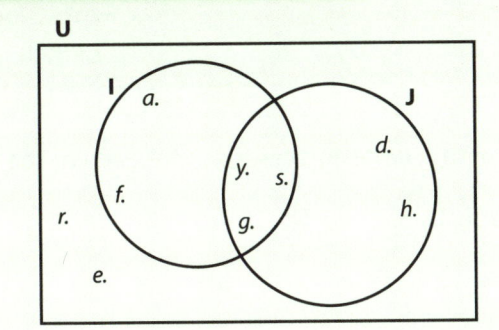
- U = #U = 9
- I = #I = 5
- I' = #I' = 4
- J = #J = 5
- J' = #J' = 4
- (I ∪ J) = #I∪J = 7
- (I ∩ J) = #I∩J = 3
- (I ∪ J)' = #I∪J' = 2
- (I ∩ J)' = #I∩J' = 6

2. 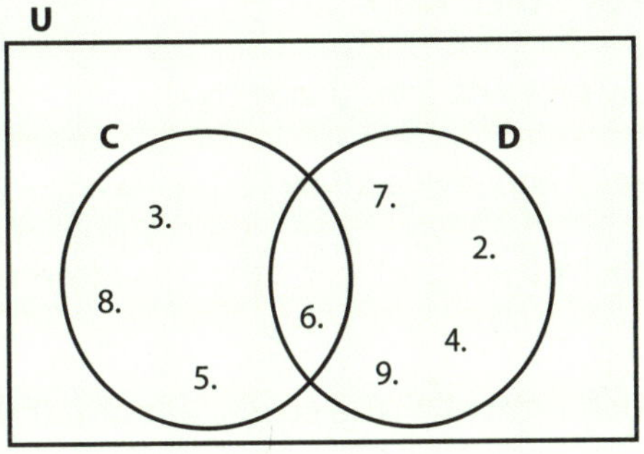
- U = ...
- C = ...
- C' = ...
- D = ...
- D' = ...
- (C ∪ D) = ...
- (C ∩ D) = ...
- (C ∪ D)' = ...
- (C ∩ D)' = ...

3. 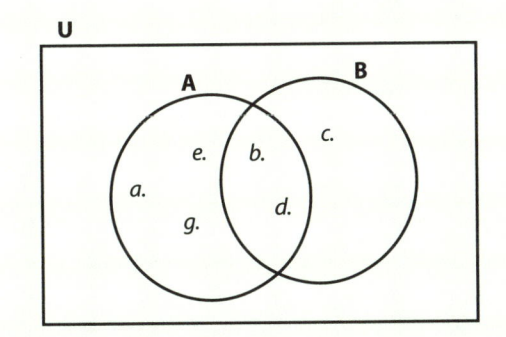
- U = #U = 6
- A = #A = 5
- B = #B = 3
- (A ∪ B) = #A∪B = 6
- (A ∪ B)' = #A∪B' = 0
- (A ∩ B) = #A∩B = 2
- (A ∩ B)' = #A∩B' = 4

Date 12/9/16   Signed ....

6.1 Algebra

> **Remember:**
> Equation : $y = 3x^2 + 4x - 2$
> Variables : y, x
> Constant : -2
> Terms : $3x^2, 4x, -2$
> Expression : $3x^2 + 4x - 2$
> Coefficients: $3, 4$

1. Starting with x, write an expression for each of the following instructions. The first one is done for you.

    (a) Multiply by 5 $5x$

    (b) Add 8

    (c) Subtract 6

    (d) Divide by 2

    (e) Multiply by 6 and then add 3

    (f) Subtract 3 and then divide by 8

    (g) Divide by 3 then add 7

    (h) Multiply by 4 and then divide by 9

    (i) Subtract 7 and divide 20 by your answer

    (j) Multiply by 5 and add 4 and then divide your answer by 6.

2. Find the coefficient of x^2, the coefficient of x and the constant term in each of the following.

	Coefficient of x^2	Coefficient of x	Constant term
$y = 3x^2 + 5x + 1$			
$y = 8x^2 - 3x - 2$			
$y = 4 + 2x - 5x^2$			
$y = 6x^2 + 12x - 4$			
$y = -3 + 6x - 4x^2$			

3. Simplify each of the following.

    (a) $2x + x + x =$

    (b) $2a + 4a + a =$

    (c) $x + 4x + 3x =$

    (d) $a + 5a + 3a =$

    (e) $5x + 3x =$

    (f) $5a + 4a + 6a =$

    (g) $7x + 7x + 3x =$

    (h) $8a + 7a =$

Date .... Signed ....

4. Simplify each of the following.

   (a) $5a + 15a + 20a =$

   (b) $7x + 4x - 3x =$

   (c) $10x + 7x - 5x =$

   (d) $12y + 4y - 6y =$

   (e) $7y + 7y + 7y =$

   (f) $5x + 5x + 5x =$

   (g) $7a + 6a - 9a =$

   (h) $12x - 4x - 6x =$

   (i) $20t - 8t - 12t =$

   (j) $12x - 10x + 4x =$

   (k) $8x - 10x =$

   (l) $4x - 6x - 3x =$

   (m) $5y - 4y - 6y =$

   (n) $8x - 9x + 5x =$

5. Simplify each of the following.

   (a) $12x + 2x + 4y + 3y =$

   (b) $3x + 2x + 5 + 9 =$

   (c) $3x + 4 + 5x + 2 =$

   (d) $4x + 5y - 3x + 2y =$

   (e) $6x + 5x - 3x + 4 =$

   (f) $6x + 7x + x - 3x =$

   (g) $8 + 3x - 4 + 2 =$

   (h) $5x + 8x - 6 - 4 =$

   (i) $5x - 3x + y + 4y =$

   (j) $3x + 8y - 6y - 10 =$

   (k) $6x + 3y - 7y + 5y =$

   (l) $5y - 3x + 4x - 7y =$

6. Simplify each of the following.

   (a) $3x + 2y - 6 + 4x + 3y + 2 =$

   (b) $5x - y + 2 + 3x - 5y + 6 =$

   (c) $x + 7y + 8 + 7x - 8g - 9 =$

   (d) $-2x + 4y - 3 + 5x - 6y + 7 =$

   (e) $6x + 6y + 6 + 3x - 2y - 8 =$

   (f) $3x - 10y - 12 - 8x - 4y - 3 =$

7. Simplify each of the following.

   (a) $3x^2 + 4x^2 =$

   (b) $8x^2 - 3x^2 =$

   (c) $5x^2 + 6x^2 =$

   (d) $10x^2 - 12x^2 =$

   (e) $7x^2 + 3x^2 =$

   (f) $-3x^2 - 4x^2 =$

   (g) $8x^2 - 8x^2 =$

   (h) $6x^2 - 3x^2 =$

Date ....   Signed ....

8. Simplify each of the following.

   (a) $3x^2 + 2x + 8 + 6x^2 + 4x + 5 =$

   (b) $5x^2 + x - 3 + 7x^2 + 6x + 8 =$

   (c) $8x^2 - 4x + 3 + 5x^2 + 7x + 5 =$

   (d) $9x^2 - 3x - 4 - x^2 - 6x - 3 =$

   (e) $6x^2 + 8x - 2 - 7x^2 - 9x + 4 =$

   (f) $-5x^2 + 3x - 4 - 3x^2 - 6x + 5 =$

   (g) $3x^2 - 10x - 8 + 6x^2 - 3x - 4 =$

6.2 Evaluation of Expressions

Find the value of each of the following expressions when $a = 2$ and $b = 3$.

Remember: $3a = 3 \times a$
$3ab = 3 \times a \times b$

1. (a) $6a + 2 =$
   (b) $4b - 3 =$
   (c) $3a + b =$
   (d) $5a + 2b =$
   (e) $7a - 10 =$
   (f) $a + b =$
   (g) $3a - 4b =$
   (h) $2a + 4 =$
   (i) $a + 3b + 2 =$
   (j) $5b - 6 =$
   (k) $3b - 6a - 4 =$
   (l) $8a - 5b =$

2. Find the value of each of the following expressions when $a = -4, b = 5$.

   (a) $4a + 2b =$
   (b) $5a - 3b =$
   (c) $3a - 2b =$
   (d) $7a - 4b =$
   (e) $8a + 6b =$
   (f) $a - 3b =$

3. Find the value of each of the following expressions when $x = 4, y = -6$.

   (a) $3x + 2y =$
   (b) $4x - y =$
   (c) $5x - 3y =$
   (d) $7x + 3y =$

Date .... Signed ....

4. Evaluate each of the following expressions when $x = 4$ and $y = -2$.

(a) $3xy = \quad 3 \times 4 \times (-2) = -24$

(b) $8xy + 2 =$

(c) $5x + 2xy =$

(d) $3x + 2y + 4 =$

(e) $5xy - 3 =$

(f) $10xy =$

Remember: $4x^2 = 4 \times x \times x$

5. Evaluate the following when $x = 2$ and $y = 7$.

(a) $4x^2 = \quad =$

(b) $3x^2 - 6 = \quad =$

(c) $2x^2 + 3 = \quad =$

(d) $y^2 - 4 = \quad =$

(e) $2xy = \quad =$

(f) $5x^2 - 10 = \quad =$

(g) $x^2 + y^2 = \quad =$

(h) $3x^2 - 2y^2 = \quad =$

6. Find the value of each of the following when $x = 4$.

(a) $x^2 + 2x - 4 = \quad =$

(b) $2x^2 + 5x + 2 = \quad =$

(c) $4x^2 - 3x + 5 = \quad =$

(d) $5x^2 - 4x - 3 = \quad =$

(e) $6x^2 - x + 8 = \quad =$

(f) $8x^2 - 7x + 4 = \quad =$

7. Find the value of each of the following when $x = -4$ and $y = 5$.

(a) $x^2 + 2x = \quad (-4)^2 + 2(-4) = 16 - 8 \quad = \quad 8$

(b) $2y^2 - 4y = \quad =$

(c) $2x^2 - y = \quad =$

(d) $4xy + y^2 = \quad =$

(e) $4x^2 - 2x = \quad =$

(f) $3y^2 - 5x = \quad =$

Date .... Signed ....

6.3 Forming Number Sentences

1. Write a number sentence for each of the following.

Remember: Let x = the number

(a) If 6 is added to a number the result is 15. $x + 6 = 15$

(b) If 4 is subtracted from a number the result is 12.

(c) If a number is doubled the result is 20.

(d) If a number is trebled and then 4 is subtracted the result is 17.

(e) If a number is halved the result is 9.

(f) If a number is halved and then 5 is added, the result is 9.

(g) 3 times a number added to 4 is 16.

(h) Take 5 from 4 times a number and the result is 35.

(i) The perimeter of this triangle measures 44 cm.
(sides: x, $x + 4$, $2x$)

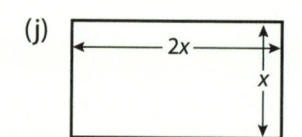

(j) The perimeter of this rectangle measures 66 cm.
(sides: $2x$, x)

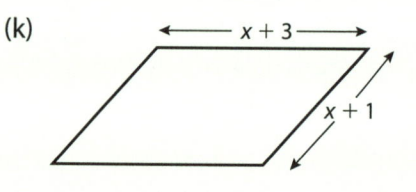

(k) The perimeter of this parallelogram measures 20 cm.
(sides: $x + 3$, $x + 1$)

(l) Half of John's age + 4 years is 10 years.

(m) John is 3 years older than Sonya. The sum of the ages is 27.   ***

(n) Michelle is half of Peter's age. The sum of their age is 27.   ***

(o) Barry had €50 saved at the start of the year.
He then had €194 at the end of the year having saved a constant amount each month.

Date ....   Signed ....

6.4 Solving Equations

1. Find the value of x in each of the following.

(a) $x + 2 = 8$

(b) $x - 4 = 5$

(c) $x - 3 = 3$

(d) $2x = 8$

(e) $\frac{x}{4} = 3$

(f) $6x = 24$

(g) $3x + 5 = 14$

(h) $4x - 2 = 38$

(i) $\frac{x}{2} + 4 = 10$

(j) $\frac{x}{5} - 2 = 6$

(k) $3x + 1 = 34$

(l) $6x + \frac{1}{2} = \frac{37}{2}$

(m) $\frac{3x}{2} = 18$

(n) $7x - 1 = 13$

(o) $\frac{5x}{3} = 20$

(p) $3x + x = 28$

(q) $2x + 4x = 18$

(r) $8x - 3x = 15$

(s) $2x + \frac{x}{2} = 10$

(t) $3x - 6 = 14$

(u) $6x + 18 = 6$

(v) $3x + 46 = 10$

(w) $\frac{x}{3} + 9 = 4$

(x) $6x - 4 = 2x$

Date .... Signed ....

2. Solve each of the following equations.

(a) $8x - 12 = 5x$

(b) $\frac{x}{4} - 2 = 6$

(c) $3x + 2 = 20$

(d) $3y + 2y + 2 = 37$

(e) $\frac{4x}{3} + \frac{2x}{3} = 10$

(f) $\frac{3x}{4} + \frac{5x}{4} = 6$

(g) $3y - 8y = 10$

(h) $5a + 4a = 54$

(i) $\frac{6x}{5} = 18$

(j) $7x + 3 = 4x + 21$

(k) $3y - 7 = 13 - 2y$

(l) $5y + y - 11 = 19$

(m) $9x - \frac{x}{3} = 78$ ***

(n) $5x + 2 = 7x - 7$

(o) $8y - 5 = 5 - 3y$

(p) $\frac{3x}{4} + 8 = x + 12$ ***

(q) $3a + 8a - 6a = 8 - a$

Date ....   Signed ....

3. (a) Write an equation for the perimeter of each shape below.
  (b) Solve your equation to find a value of x.
  (c) Use the value of x to find the length of each side.
  (d) Check that the lengths of the sides add to the length of the perimeter.

(a) Perimeter = 26 cm, width = $2x - 5$, length = $4x$

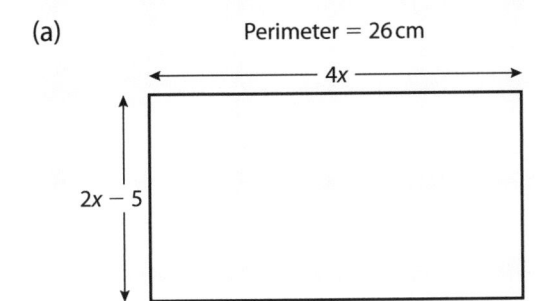

a) Equation:
$(2x - 5) + 4x + (2x - 5) + 4x = 26$

b) $12x - 10 = 26$
$12x = 26 + 10$
$12x = 36$
$\therefore x = \left(\frac{36}{12}\right) = 3$ cm

c) $4x = 4 \times 3 = 12$ cm (Length)
$2x - 5 = 2 \times 3 - 5 = 1$ cm (Width)

d) $12 + 1 + 12 + 1 = 26 \ldots$ True

(b) Perimeter = 50 cm, length = $2p - 6$, width = $p + 1$

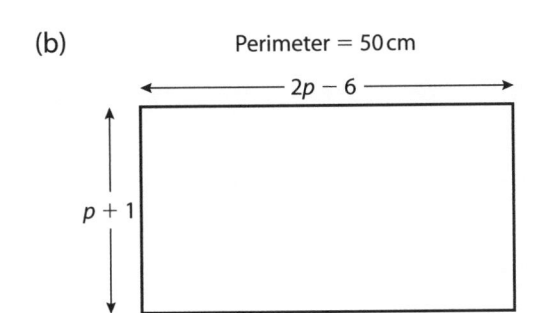

a) Equation:
$ = 50$

b)
$\therefore p =$

c) $2p - 6 =$
$p + 1 =$

d) $ = 50$

(c) Perimeter = 94 cm, width = $x - 5$, length = $4x + 2$

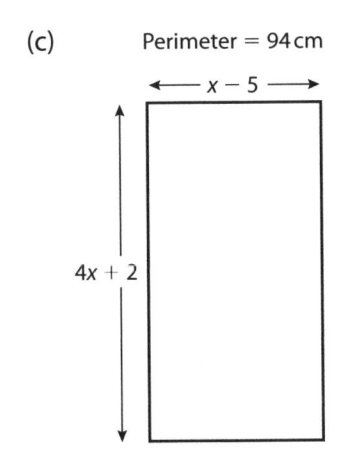

a) Equation:
$ = 94$

b)
$\therefore x =$

c) $x - 5 =$
$4x + 2 =$

d)

Date .... Signed ....

(d) Perimeter = 56 cm

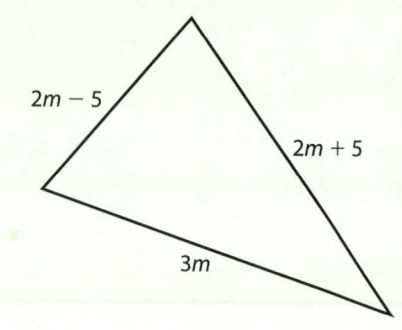

2m − 5
2m + 5
3m

a) Equation:

b)

$\therefore m =$

c) 2m − 5 =
2m + 5 =
3m   =

d)

(e) Perimeter = 34 cm

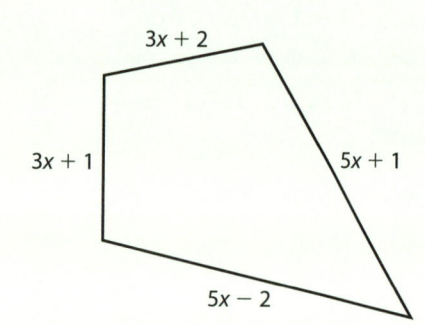

3x + 2
3x + 1
5x + 1
5x − 2

a) Equation:

b)

$\therefore x =$

c) 3x + 1 =
3x + 2 =
5x + 1 =
5x − 2 =

d)

(f) Perimeter = 46 cm

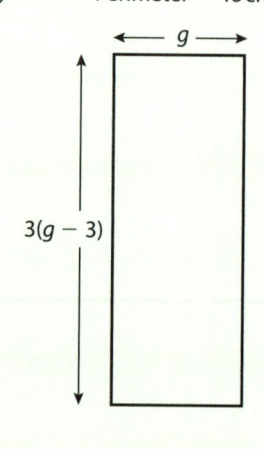

g
3(g − 3)

a) Equation:

b)

$\therefore g =$

c) g =
3(g − 3) =

d)

Date ....   Signed ....

4. Find the size of each angle in the following triangles.

Remember: All 3 angles in a triangle add to 180°.

(a)

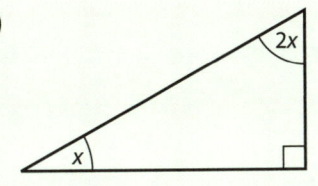

                               = 180°

∴ $x =$
∴ $2x =$

(b)

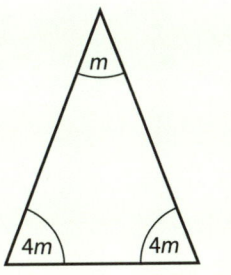

                               = 180°

∴ $m =$
∴ $4m =$

(c)

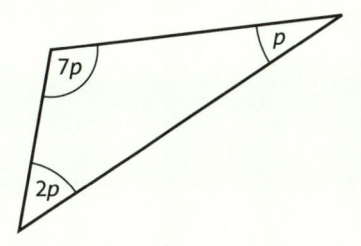

                               =

∴ $p =$
∴ $2p =$
∴ $7p =$

(d)

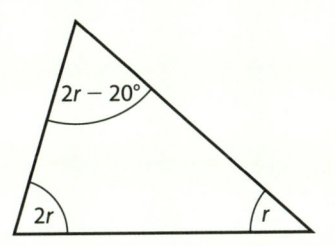

                               =

∴ $r =$
∴ $2r =$
∴ $2r - 20 =$
         =

(e)

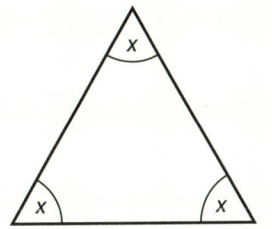

$3x =$

$x =$

Date .... Signed ....

7.1 Perimeter and Area

> **Perimeter** is the length of a boundary.
> **Area** is a measure of the surface inside a boundary.

Find the length of the perimeter and area of each of the following.

1. 12 cm, 6 cm

Perimeter = 6 + 12 + 6 + 12 = 36 cm
Area = 6 cm × 12 cm = 72 cm²

2. 14 cm, 4 cm

Perimeter = =
Area = =

3. 12 cm, 6 cm, ( )? cm, ( )? cm, 2 cm, 8 cm

(Note: Find the missing lengths first)
Perimeter = =
Area = =

4. ( )? cm, 8 cm, 12 cm, 6 cm, ( )? cm, 4 cm

Perimeter = =
Area = =

5. 6 cm, 4 cm, 6 cm, 12 cm, ( )? cm, ( )? cm, 2 cm, ( )? cm

Perimeter = =
Area = =

6. 12 cm, 10 cm, 16 cm, 12 cm

Perimeter = =
Area = =

***

Date .... Signed ....

7.2 Area of Triangles

Remember:
Area = $\frac{1}{2} \times l \times h$

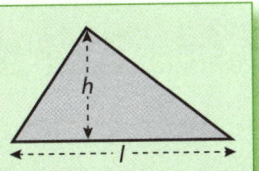

Find the area of each of the following (shaded) triangles.

1.
8 cm, 18 cm

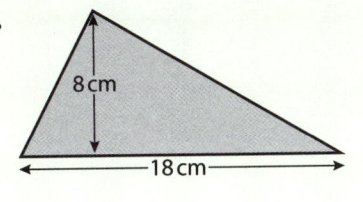

Area =
=

2.
10 cm, 22 cm

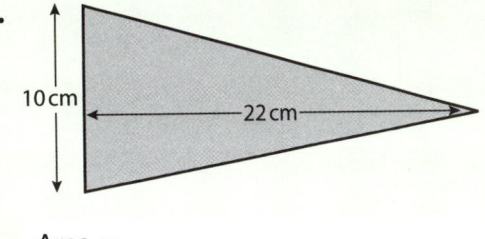

Area =
=

3.
14 cm, 8 cm

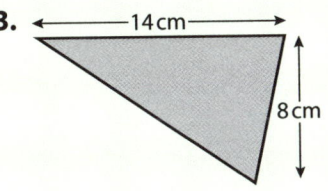

Area =
=

4.
10 cm, 16 cm

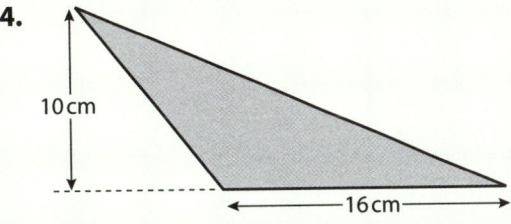

Area =
=

5.
10 cm, 20 cm

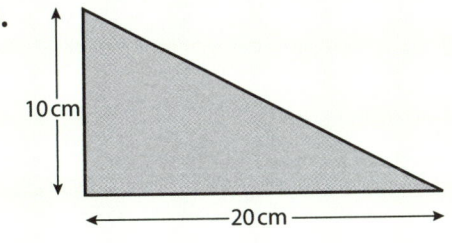

Area =
=

6.
9 cm, 26 cm

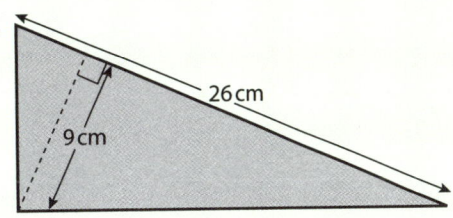

Area =
=

7.
12 cm, 6 cm, 10 cm

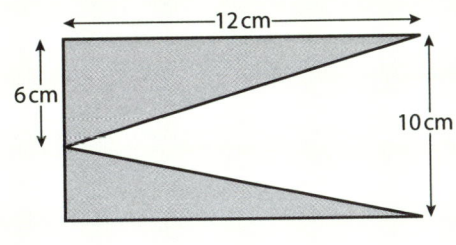

Area =
=

8.
8 cm, 8 cm, 10 cm

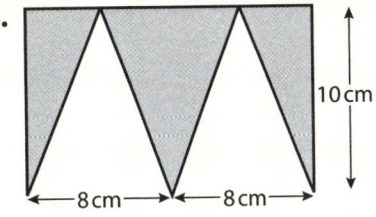

Area =
=

***

Date ....   Signed ....

7.3 Challenging Area + Perimeter Questions

Find the length of the perimeter of each of the shapes A and B.

9.

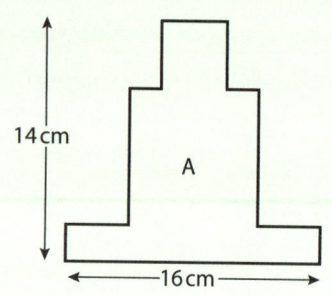

Perimeter A =

Perimeter B =

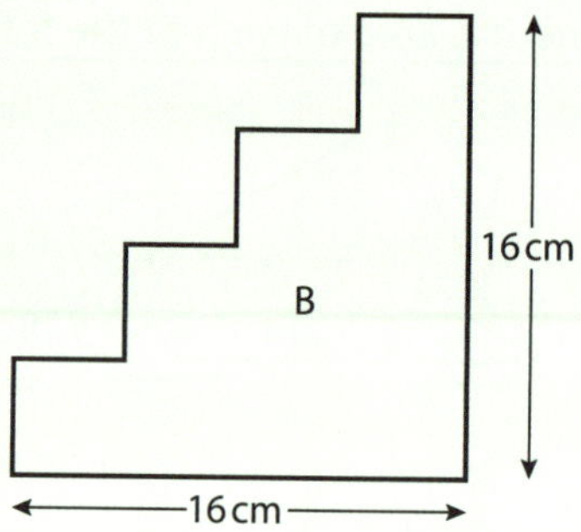

Find the area of each of the shaded sections.

10.

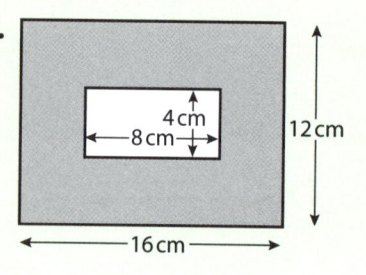

Area =   ***

11.

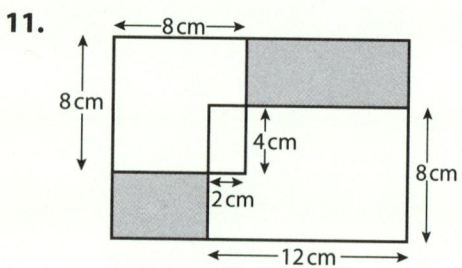

Area =   ***

12.

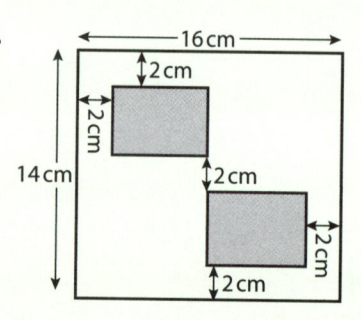

Area =   ***

13.

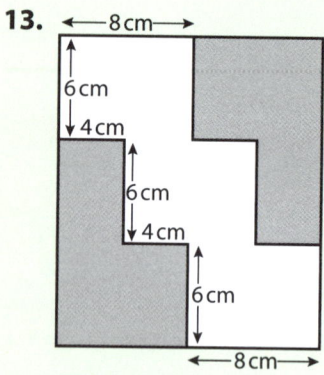

Area =   ***

Date ....   Signed ....

8.1 Proportion

Example: What proportion of this shape is shaded?

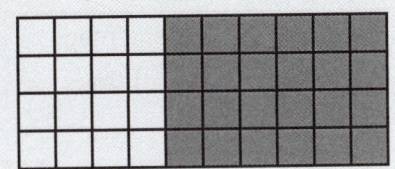

$\frac{24}{40} = \frac{3}{5} = 0.6 = 60\%$

Remember: A proportion can be expressed as a fraction, a decimal or a percentage.

1. (a) Which diagram has the greater number of coloured squares?

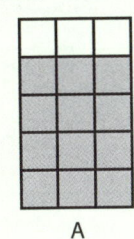

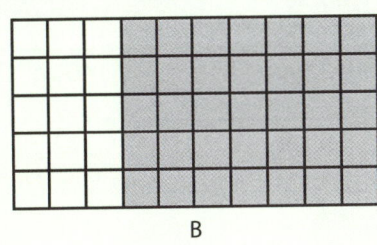

   A   B

   (b) Which diagram has the greater proportion of coloured squares?

   (c) Find the proportion of coloured squares in each diagram as (i) a fraction (ii) a percentage.

Coloured squares	A	B
Fraction		
Percentage		

2. In a football match Team A had 25 shots at goal, 17 on target
   Team B had 18 shots at goal, 12 on target.

   (a) Find the proportion of shots on target for each team   (i) as a fraction
   (ii) as a percentage

On target	Team A	Team B
Fraction		
Percentage		

   (b) Which team is the more accurate?

3. (a) Nine out of twenty students of a class are girls.
   Find the proportion of boys in the same class as a percentage.   %

   (b) 85% of the same class are right-handed.
   Find the proportion of left-handed students in the same class as

   (i) a percentage   %

   (ii) a fraction

   (c) Three of the girls and two of the boys are brown-eyed.
   Write the proportion of brown-eyed students in the class as a percentage.   %

   (d) What proportion of the girls are (give your answer as a fraction).

   (i) brown-eyed

   (ii) not brown-eyed

Date ....   Signed ....

4. The following table compares Body Mass with Brain Mass for a range of different animals. Compare the table finding the proportion of Brain Mass to Body Mass as
   (i) a fraction in its lowest terms   (ii) as a percentage

(a)

Species	Brain Mass	Body Mass	Proportion Fraction	Proportion Percentage
Dolphin	1700 g	170,000 g	$\frac{1700}{170,000} = \frac{1}{100}$	1.0%
Elephant	4000 g	4,000,000 g		
Horse	420 g	350,000 g		
Human	1400 g	70,000 g		
Rabbit	12 g	2400 g		
Rat	2.5 g	200 g		

(b) List the percentages in order, highest first.

Percentage	Species

(c) Is brain mass to body mass ratio a good way to compare intelligence?

Explain

8.2 Direct Proportion

1. €10 is worth $13. How much is €20 worth?

2. 3 packets of crisps cost €1.20. How much will 12 packets cost?

3. 3 pies cost €9.00. How much will 2 pies cost?

4. 3 Easter eggs cost €1.60. How much will 15 eggs cost?

5. 5 miles is about 8 km.

   Convert 20 miles into kilometers.

   Convert 24 km into miles.

6. If 500 g of chicken is needed to make a chicken curry for 2 people, how much chicken is needed to make a chicken curry for 3 people?

Date ....   Signed ....

8.3 Ratio

> If there are 20 discs in a bag, 8 of which are red and 12 blue, then the ratio of red to blue is said to be
> 8 : 12 (read, eight "is to" twelve
> 2 : 3 (for every two red, there are three blue)

1. Write each of the following ratios in their simplest form.

   (a) 5 : 15   1 : 3   (b) 27 : 9   (c) 8 : 24

   (d) 45 : 30   (e) 7 : 28   (f) 8 : 56

   (g) 18 : 81   (h) 11 : 132   (i) 100 : 240

2. Fill in the missing gaps.

   (a) 1 : 2 =   3 :   (b) 3 : 9 =   : 3   (c) 1 : 4 =   2 :

   (d) 1 : 5 =   5 :   (e) 6 : 30 =   2 :   (f) 3 : 5 =   : 25

   (g) 10 : 4 =   5 :   (h) 9 : 12 =   6 :   (i) 100 : 5 =   : 1

3. (a) Shade this bar in the ratio 3 : 7.
   (b) Shade this bar in the ratio 6 : 4.
   (c) Shade this bar in the ratio 3 : 2.
   (d) Shade this bar in the ratio 8 : 32.

4. Write each of the following ratio in their simplest form.

   (a) 25 cm : 1 m   25 : 100   (b) 10 cm : 1 mm   :
       ⇒ 1 : 4   ⇒   :

   (c) €1 : 20 c   :   (d) 1 km : 500 m   :
       ⇒   :   ⇒   :

   (e) 40 mm : 3 cm   :   (f) 200 g : 1 kg   :
       ⇒   :   ⇒   :

   (g) €1.35 : €2.70   :   (h) 16 cm : 1 m   :   ***
       ⇒   :   ⇒   :

5. Change each of the following into their simplest form.

   (a) $1\frac{1}{2}$: 2 =   :   (b) 3 : $\frac{1}{4}$ =   :

   (c) $2\frac{1}{5}$: 3 =   :   (d) 4.5 : 1.5 =   :

   (e) 2.1 : 3 =   :   (f) $3\frac{1}{3}$: 2 =   :

         =   :   =   :

   Remember: Ratios in their simplest form must not contain fractions or decimals.

   Date ....   Signed ....

8.4 Changing Ratios to Proportions

Remember: Ratios compare part to part. **Proportions** compare part to whole.

1. Change each of the following ratios to proportions.

   (a) Cats : Dogs   Cats, Dogs
       3 : 4   = $\frac{3}{7}, \frac{4}{7}$

   (b) Boys : Girls   Boys, Girls
       7 : 13   =

   (c) Blue : Red   Blue, Red
       8 : 7   =

   (d) Sweets : Drinks   Sweets, Drinks
       20 : 36   =

   (e) Dancers : Singers   Dancers, Singers
       32 : 88   =

   (f) Fruit : Cake   Fruit, Cake
       6 : 5   =

2. Divide €540 in the ratio 6 : 3. $6 : 3 = \frac{6}{9}, \frac{3}{9}$
   $\Rightarrow \frac{6}{9} \times €540 = €360$ and $\frac{3}{9}$ of €540 = €180

3. Divide €420 in the ratio 3 : 7.   3 : 7 =
   $\Rightarrow$ ( ) × €420 =   and ( ) × €420 =

4. Divide €720 in the ratio 5 : 4.   5 : 4 =
   $\Rightarrow$ ( ) × €720 =   and ( ) × €720 =

5. Divide €182 in the ratio 4 : 3.   4 : 3 =
   $\Rightarrow$ ( ) × €182 =   and ( ) × €182 =

6. Divide €374 in the ratio 6 : 5.

9. Divide €338 in the ratio 10 : 3.

7. Divide €247 in the ratio 6 : 7.

10. Divide €264 in the ratio 5 : 17.

8. Divide €1166 in the ratio 4 : 7.

11. Divide €560 in the ratio 9 : 5.

Date ....   Signed ....

12. Find the
(a) Ratio
(b) proportion of shaded to unshaded in each of the following.

(i)

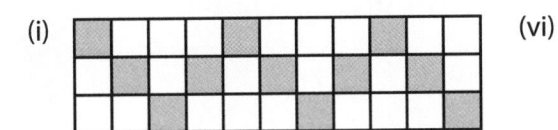

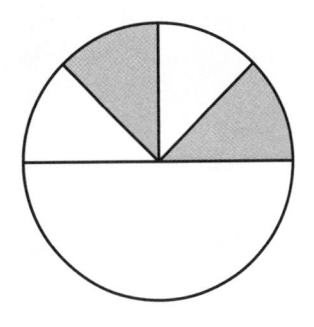

        Shaded : Unshaded
  (a) Ratio   :
  (b) Proportion   ,

(ii)

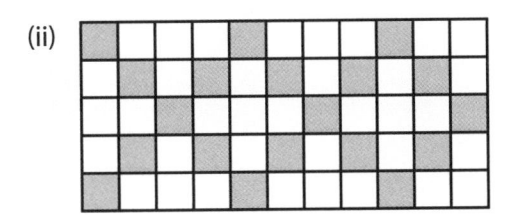

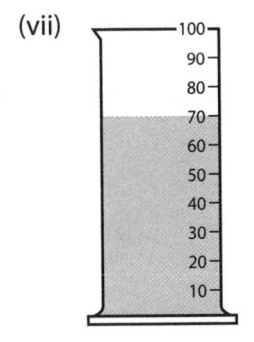

        Shaded : Unshaded
  (a) Ratio   :
  (b) Proportion   ,

(iii)

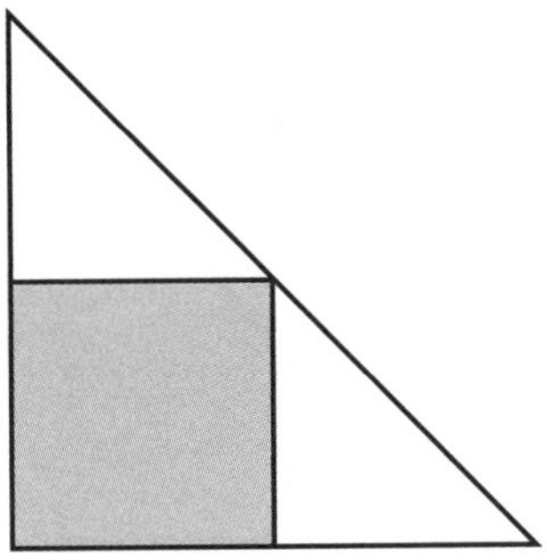

        Shaded : Unshaded
  (a) Ratio   :
  (b) Proportion   ,

(iv)

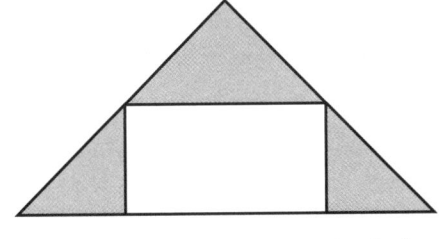

        Shaded : Unshaded
  (a) Ratio   :
  (b) Proportion   ,

(v)

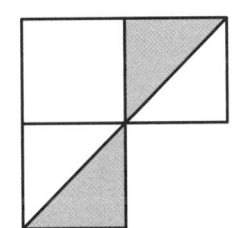

        Shaded : Unshaded
  (a) Ratio   :
  (b) Proportion   ,

(vi)

        Shaded : Unshaded
  (a) Ratio   :
  (b) Proportion   ,

(vii)

        Shaded : Unshaded
  (a) Ratio   :
  (b) Proportion   ,

(viii)

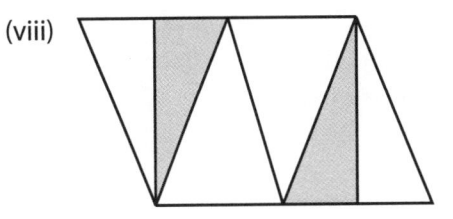

        Shaded : Unshaded
  (a) Ratio   :
  (b) Proportion   ,

(ix)

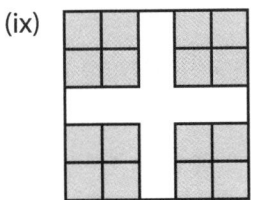

        Shaded : Unshaded
  (a) Ratio   :
  (b) Proportion   ,

Date .... Signed ....

9.1 Angles

1. Label each of the angles below using the terms, acute, obtuse, reflex, straight, right-angled. (One term is used twice.)

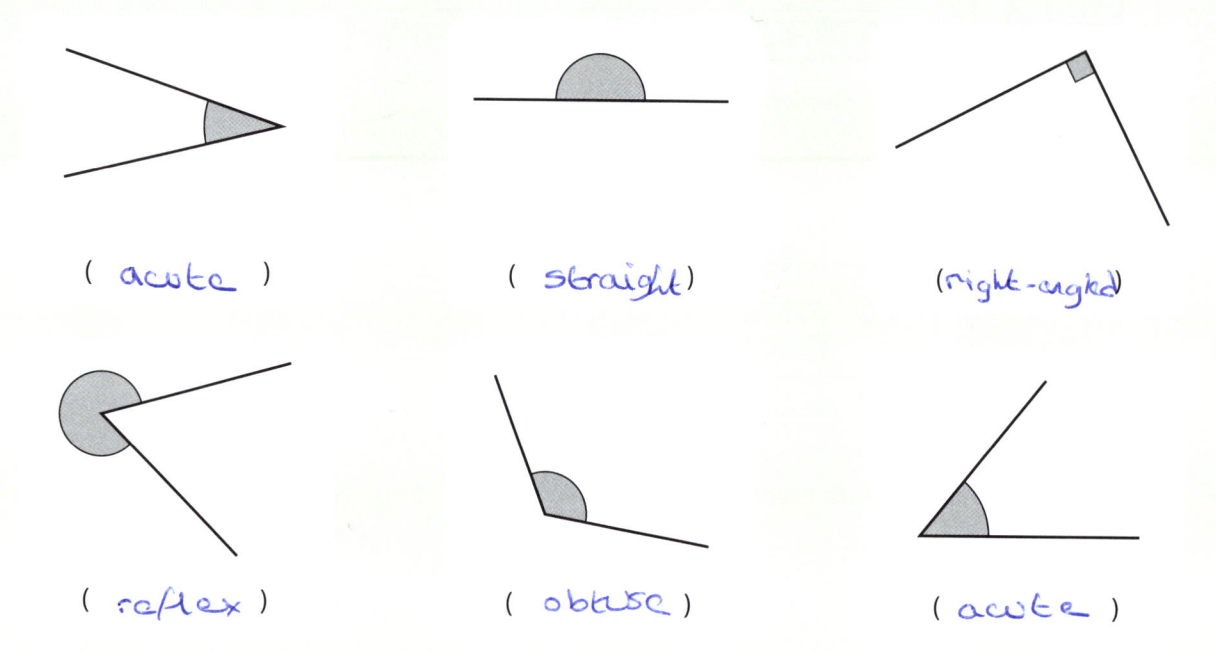

(acute)   (straight)   (right-angled)

(reflex)   (obtuse)   (acute)

2. Measuring angles

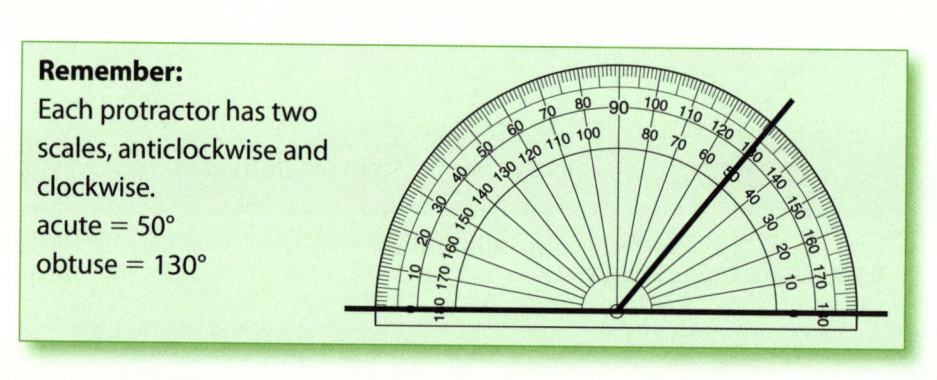

Remember:
Each protractor has two scales, anticlockwise and clockwise.
acute = 50°
obtuse = 130°

(a) Each of the following diagrams shows one arm of an angle. Given the type of angle being measured, read the scale to find the size of each angle.

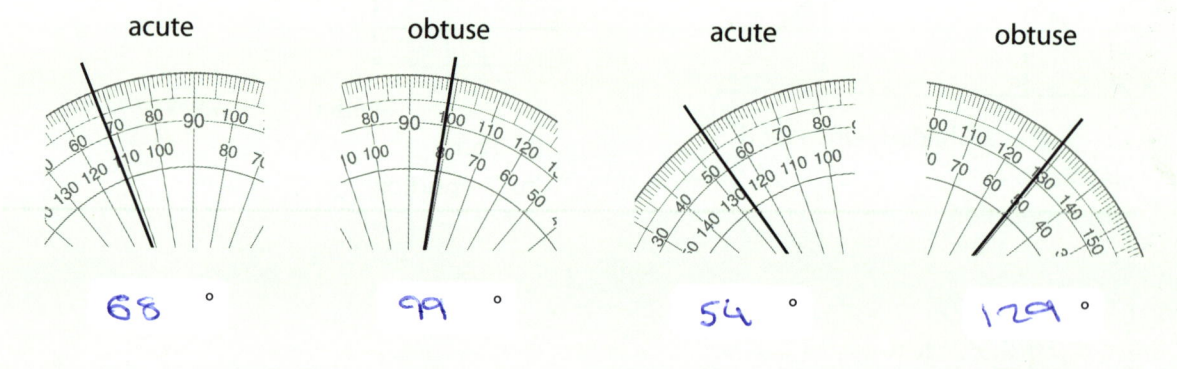

acute — 68°

obtuse — 99°

acute — 54°

obtuse — 129°

Date ....   Signed ....

(b) Given the type of angle, read the scale to find the size of the angle.

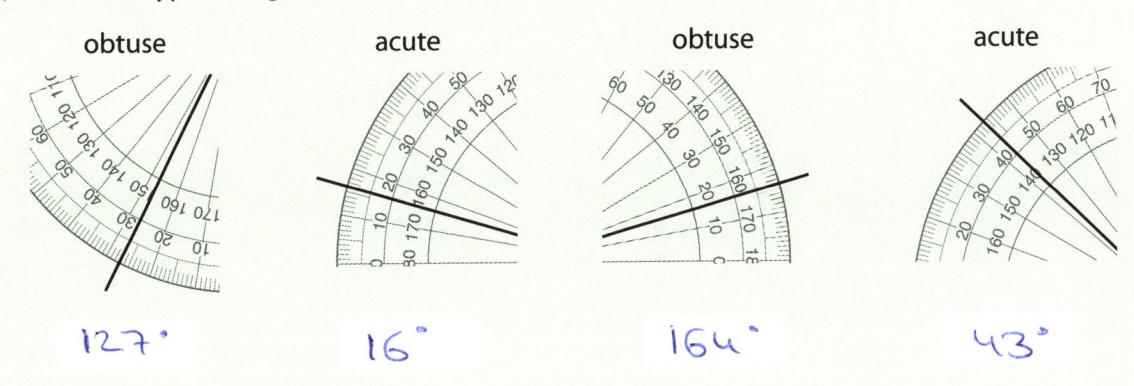

obtuse   acute   obtuse   acute

127°   16°   164°   43°

(c) A 360° protractor was used to measure a reflex angle below. Find the size of the angle.

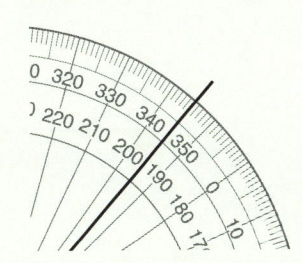

Remember:
A circular protractor can measure up to 360°.

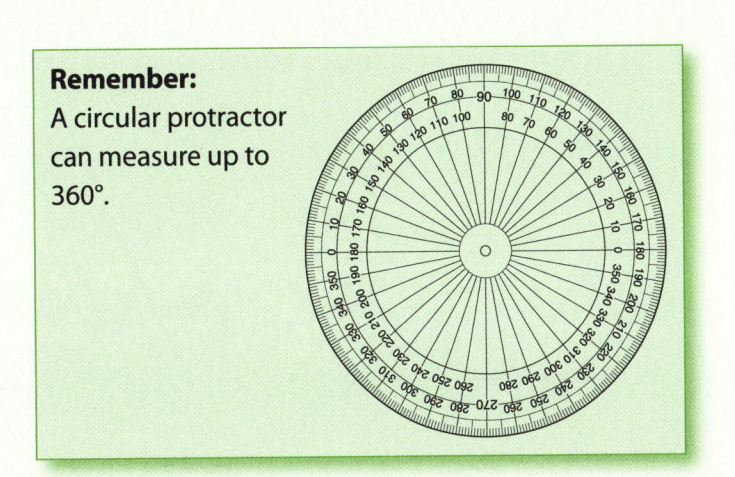

(d) Use the information given on these diagrams to find the unknown angles.

(i) Obtuse

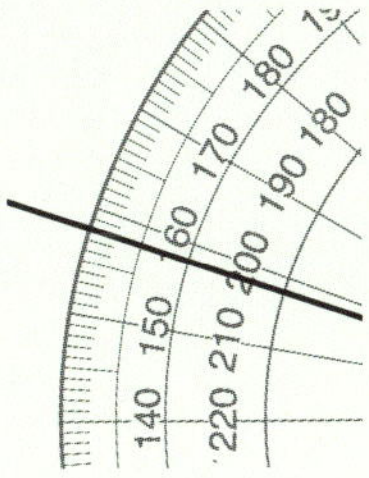

(ii) Reflex

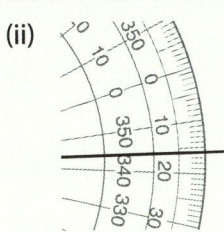

(iii) Obtuse

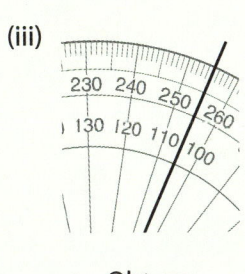

(iv) Reflex

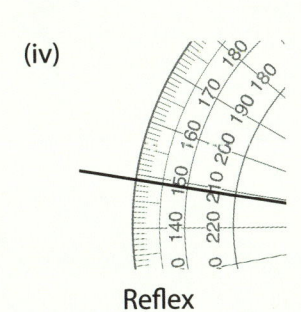

Date .... Signed ....

3. In each of the following find the size of the reflex angle.

Remember: A full turn = 360°.

(a) 60°

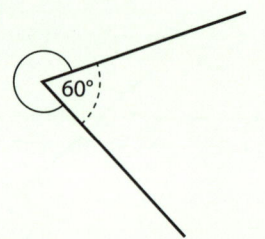

(b) 30°

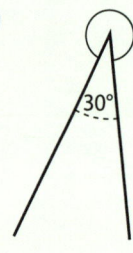

(c) 105°

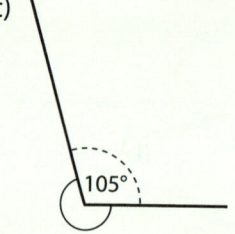

(d)

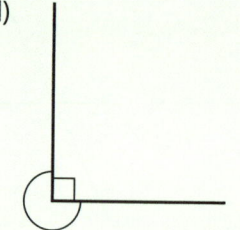

4. Measure the following angles, accurately using a protractor.

(a)

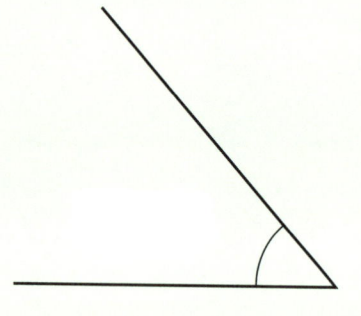

(b)

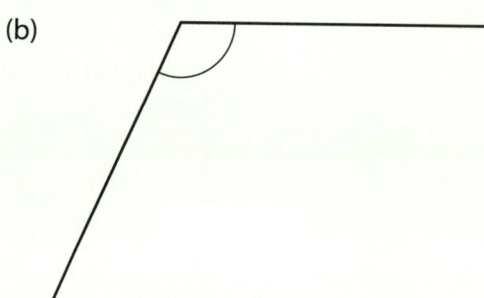

(c)

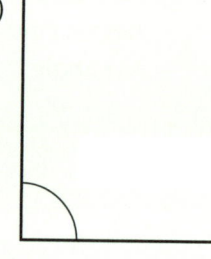

(d)

(e)

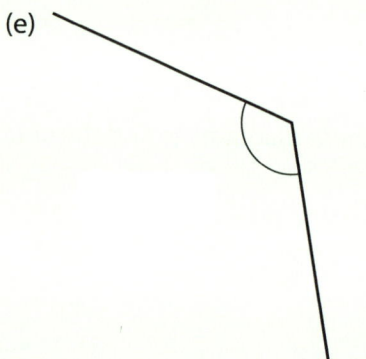

(f)

(g)

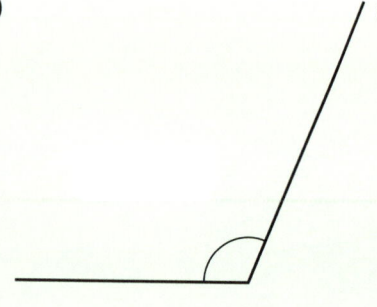

(h)

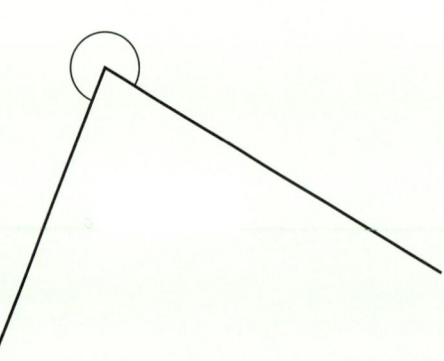

(i)

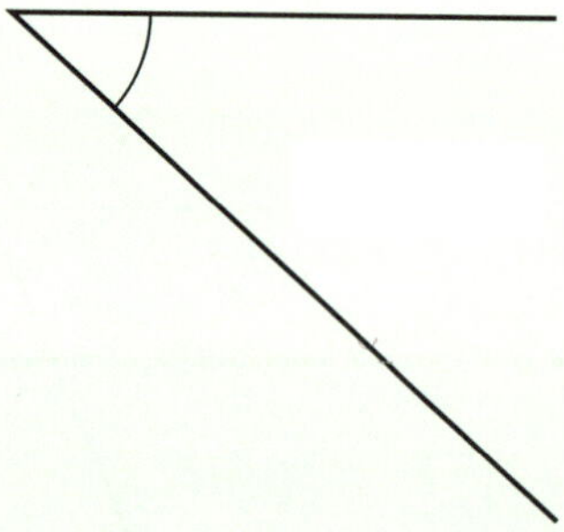

Date ....   Signed ....

9.2 Geometry I

Remember:

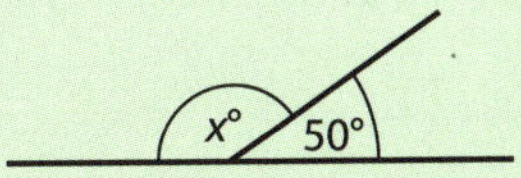

$x = 180° - 50°$
$x = 130°$

1. Find the value of x in each of the following.

(a)

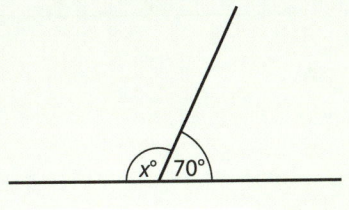

$x° + 70° = 180°$
$\Rightarrow x =$
$x =$

(b)

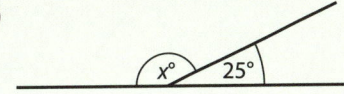

$x =$

(c)

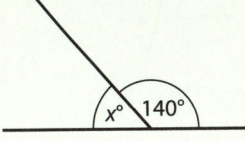

$x =$

2. Find the value of $x°$ and $y°$ in each of the following.

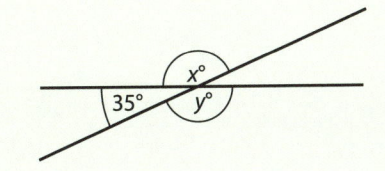

$x =$
$y =$

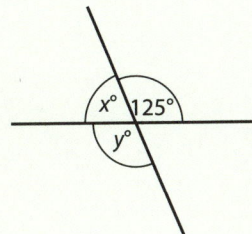

$x =$
$y =$

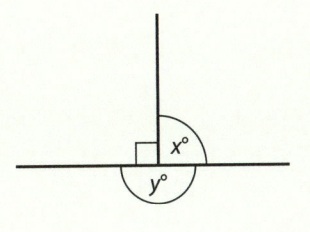

$x =$
$y =$

3. Find the value of x in each of the following.

(a)

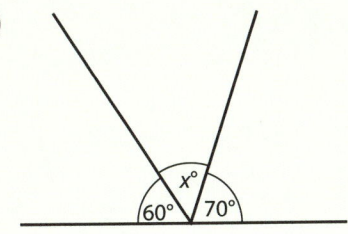

$x =$

(b)

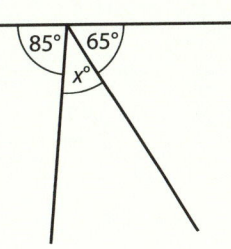

$x =$

(c)

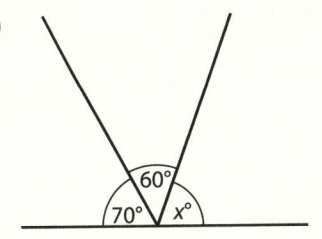

$x =$

Date .... Signed ....

4. Find the size of the angles marked with a letter.

(i)

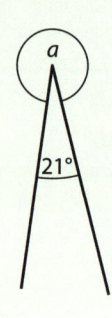

a =

(ii)

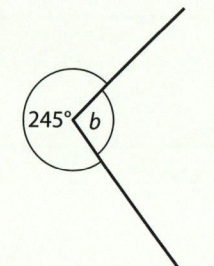

b =

(iii)

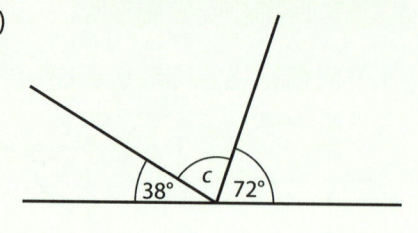

c =

(iv)

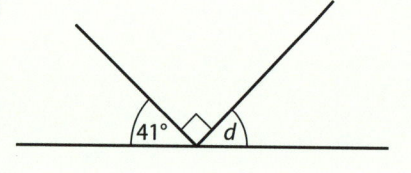

d =

(v)

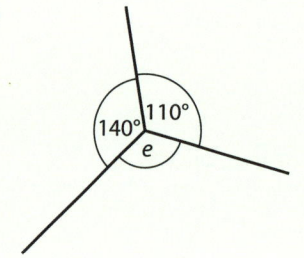

e =

(vi)

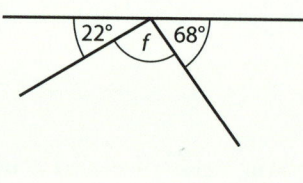

f =

(vii)

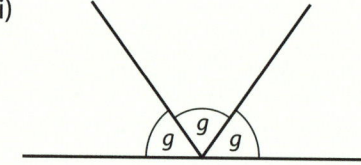

g =

(viii)

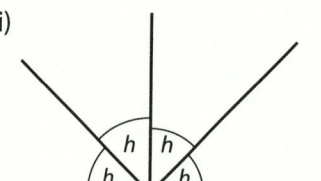

h =

(ix)

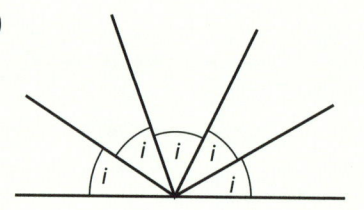

i =

(x)

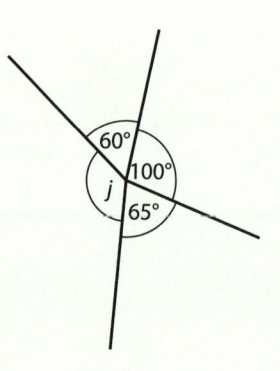

j =

(xi)

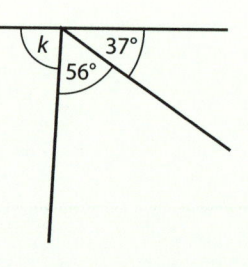

k =

(xii)

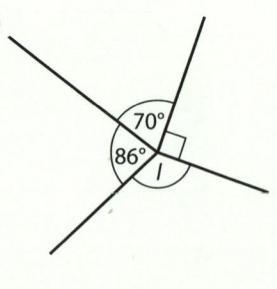

l =

Date .... Signed ....

5. Calculate the size of the angles marked by a letter.

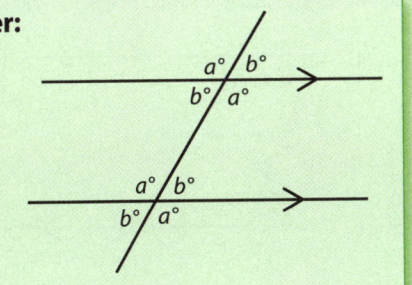

(i)

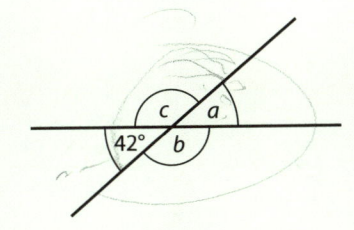

a = 42° ✓
b = 138° ✓
c = 138° ✓

Remember:

(ii)

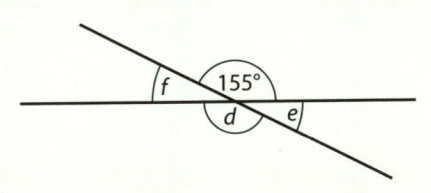

d = 155° ✓
e = 25° ✓
f = 25° ✓

(iii)

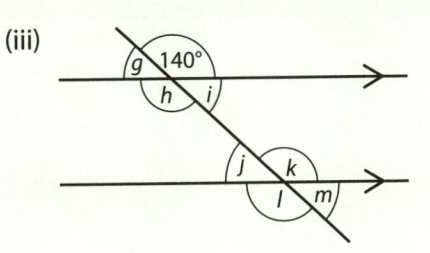

g = 40° ✓
h = 140° ✓
i = 40° ✓
j = 40° ✓
k = 140° ✓
l = 140° ✓
m = 40° ✓

(iv)

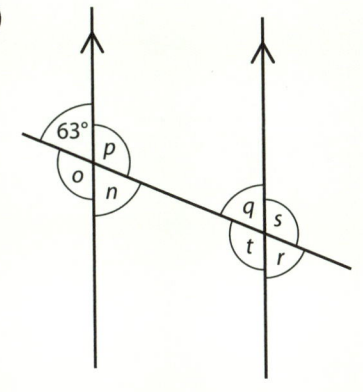

n = 63° ✓
o = 117° ✓
p = 117° ✓
q = 63° ✓
r = 63° ✓
s = 117° ✓
t = 117° ✓

(v)

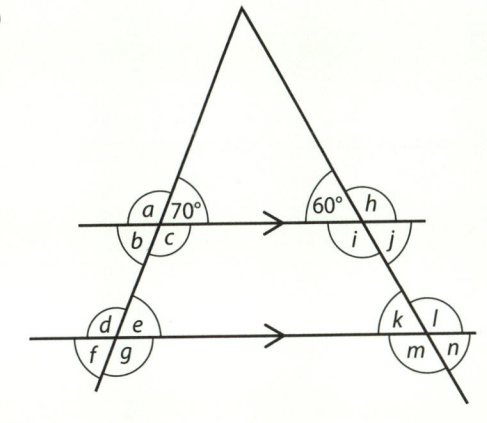

a = 110° ✓   h = 120° ✓
b = 70° ✓   i = 120° ✓
c = 110° ✓   j = 60° ✓
d = 110° ✓   k = 60° ✓
e = 70° ✓   l = 120° ✓
f = 70° ✓   m = 120° ✓
g = 110° ✓   n = 60° ✓

Date .... Signed ....

6. Find the size of the angles marked by a letter.

(i)

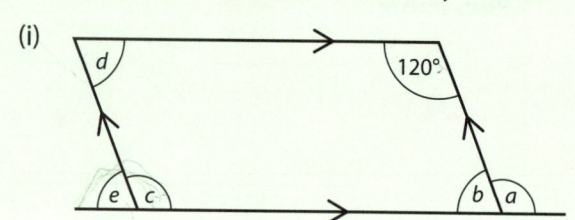

a = 120°
b = 60°
c = 120°
d = 60°
e = 60°

(ii)

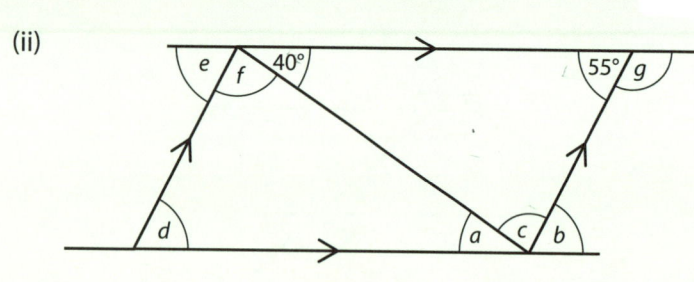

a = 40°
b = 55°
c = 85°
d = 55°
e = 55°
f = 85°
g = 125°

(iii)

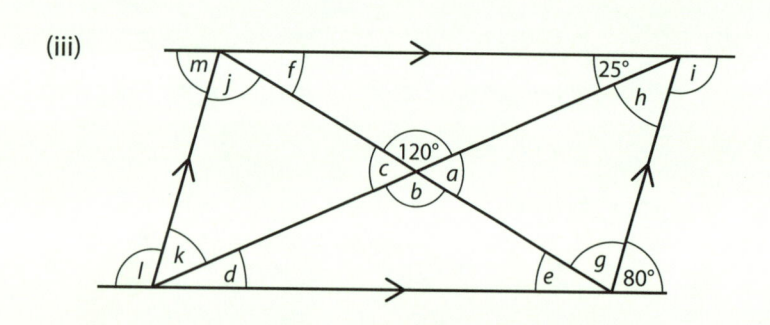

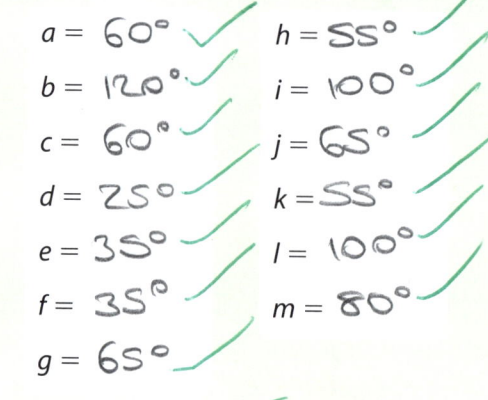

a = 60°   h = 55°
b = 120°   i = 100°
c = 60°   j = 65°
d = 25°   k = 55°
e = 35°   l = 100°
f = 35°   m = 80°
g = 65°

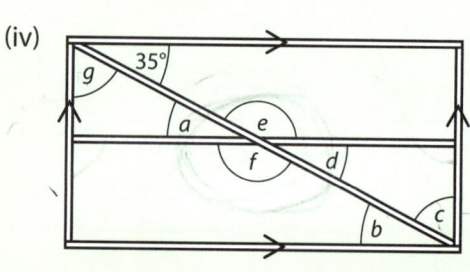

(iv)

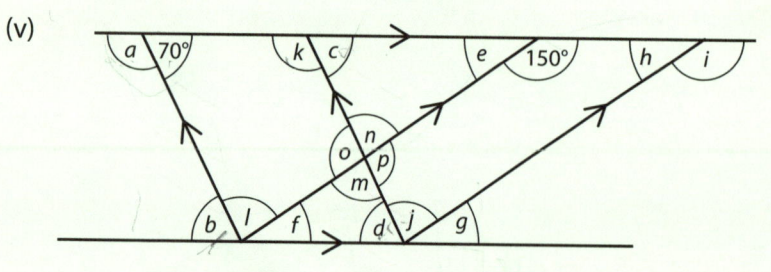

a = 35°   e = 145°
b = 35°   f = 145°
c = 55°   g = 55°
d = 35°

(v)

a = 110°   i = 150°
b = 70°   j = 80°
c = 70°   k = 110°
d = 70°   l = 80°
e = 30°   m = 80°
f = 30°   n = 80°
g = 30°   o = 100°
h = 30°   p = 100°

Date .... Signed ....

9.3 Geometry II

Remember: 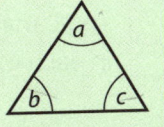
$a° + b° + c° = 180°$

1. Calculate the size of the 3rd angle in each triangle.

(a) [90°, 45°, a]

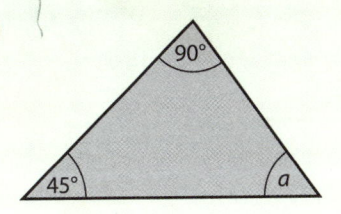

$a = 45°$

(b) [b, 48°, 38°]

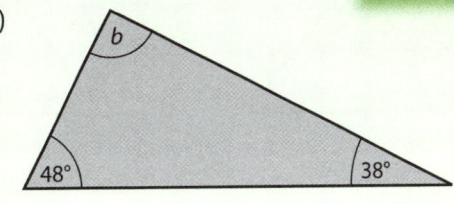

$b = 94°$

(c) [60°, 50°, c]

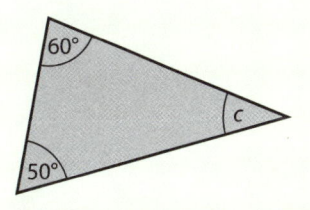

$c = 70°$

(d) [24°, 88°, d]

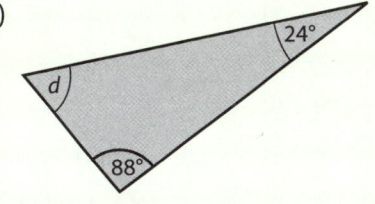

$d = 68°$

(e) [28°, 50°, e, f, right angle]

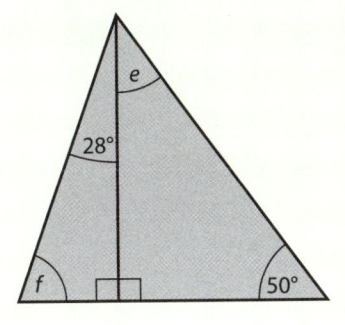

$e = 40°$ $f = 62°$

(f) [26°, g, h, 120°, 25°, i]

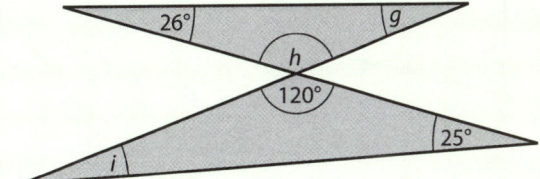

$g = 34°$
$h = 120°$
$i = 35°$

(g) [110°, 70°, j, 30°, 30°, k]

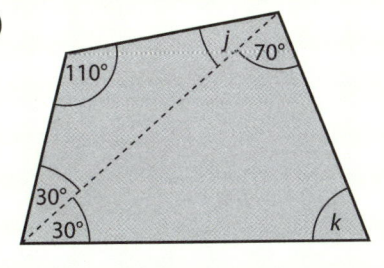

$j = 40°$
$k = 80°$

Date ....   Signed ....

1. Calculate the size of the angle marked by a letter in each of the following.

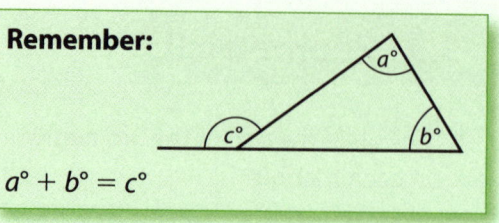

Remember:
$a° + b° = c°$

(a)

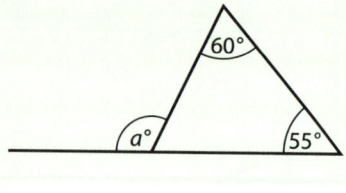

a =   +

a° =

(b)

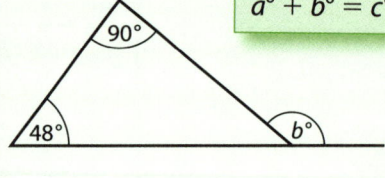

b =   +

b° =

(c)

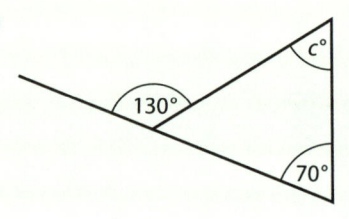

c + 70 =

c° =

(d)

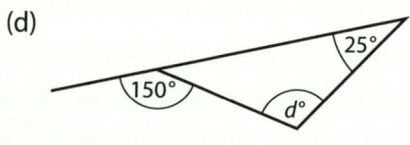

d +   = 150

d° =

(e)

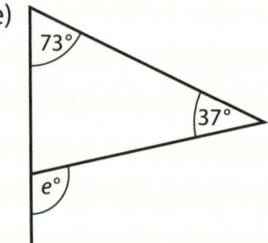

e =

(f)

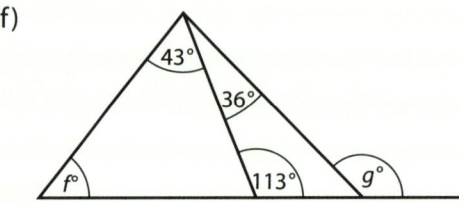

f° =

g° =

(g)

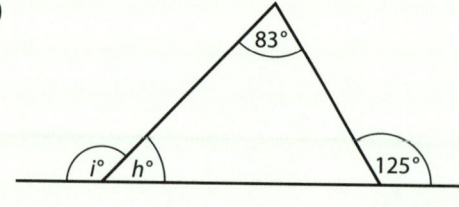

h° =

i° =

(h)

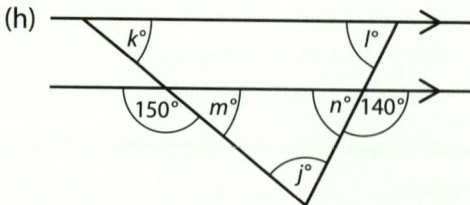

m° =   n° =

j° =   l° =

k° =

Date ....   Signed ....

3. Use the information of the last three sections to calculate the size of the missing angles.

(a)

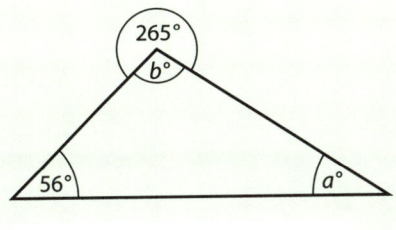

$a° =$

$b° =$

(b)

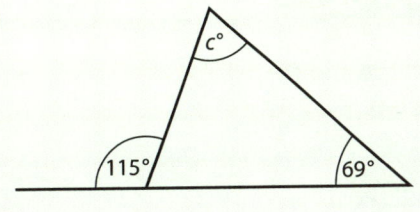

$c° =$

(c)

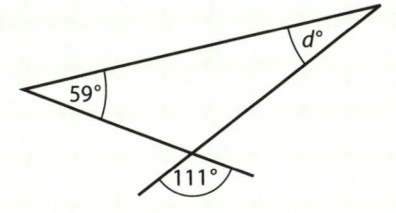

$d° =$

(d) Note: $3e = e + e + e$

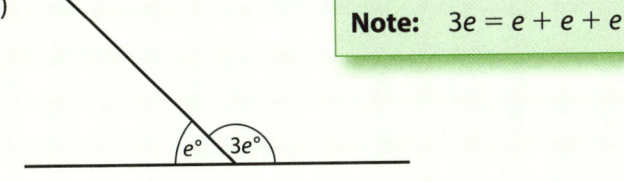

$e° =$

(e)

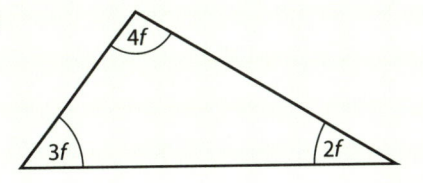

$f° =$

(f)

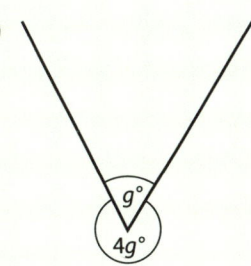

$g° =$

(g)

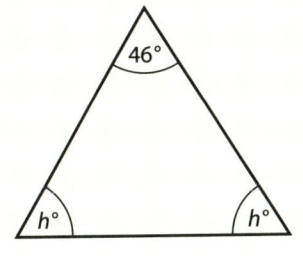

$h° =$

(h)

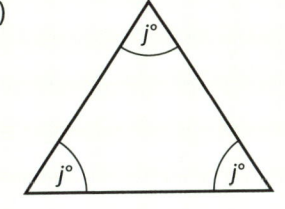

$j° =$

Date .... Signed ....

9.4 Geometry III

Remember:

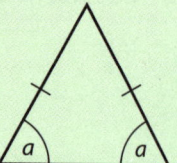

1. Find the size of the angles marked with a letter.

(a)

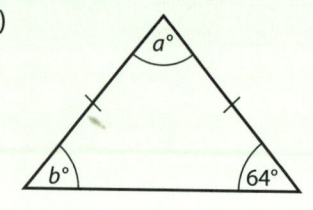

$a° =$
$b° =$

(b)

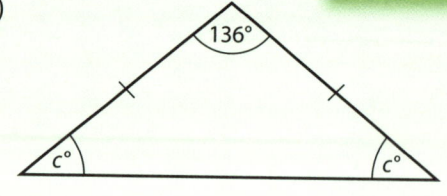

$c° =$

(c)

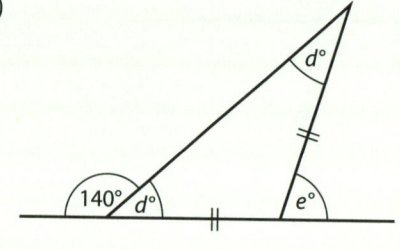

$d° =$
$e° =$

(d)

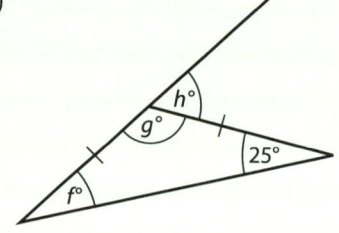

$f° =$
$g° =$
$h° =$

(e)

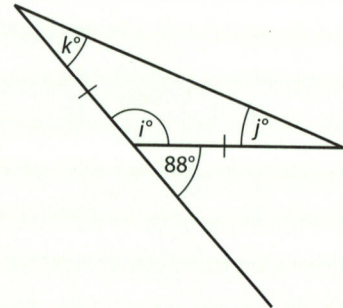

$i° =$
$j° =$
$k° =$

(f)

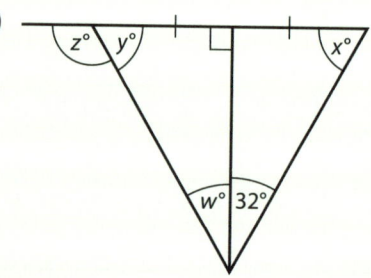

$w° =$
$x° =$
$y° =$
$z° =$

Date .... Signed ....

10.1 Statistics – Collecting data

1. Rearrange these terms into the correct order.

Analyse the data	1.
Present the data	2.
Pose a question	3.
Collect the data	4.

2. Collecting data:
List the advantages and disadvantages of each of the following methods of collecting data.

	Advantages	Disadvantages
1. Using the <u>internet</u> to hold your survey		
2. <u>Posting</u> a questionnaire to individual people		
3. Asking questions <u>face to face</u>		
4. <u>Telephoning</u> people and reading them the questions		

3. Using the terms – <u>Unclear</u> – <u>Too personal</u> – <u>Embarrassing</u> – <u>Too leading</u> – <u>Biased</u> – <u>Upsetting or offensive</u>, say why each of the following questions would not be suitable.

(a) What do you think about young people?	
(b) How old are you?	
(c) Don't you agree that people drink too much alcohol?	
(d) Why do you think that women drivers are better than men?	
(e) What are your opinions on the state of the economy?	
(f) What qualifications do you have?	
(g) Most students want less homework. Do you agree?	
(h) How much money do you earn?	
(i) Are you in favour of making animals suffer to help medical research?	

Date ....   Signed ....

4. Discuss the following issues in a group.
Write down 3 questions that might be asked about each one.

(a) A student council is asked to put forward suggestions for a new school uniform. They decide to give a questionnaire to the students.

Q1.

Q2.

Q3.

(b) A group of parents want to open a youth club in a local hall.
They decide to do a survey of local opinion.

Q1.

Q2.

Q3.

(c) An anti-bullying policy is to be drawn up in a school. The student council survey the students so as to contribute to the policy. What questions should be asked?

Q1.

Q2.

Q3.

(d) The teachers in a school want to be able to use computers to assign homework. They survey the students on computer use at home.

Q1.

Q2.

Q3.

(e) To try to improve the understanding of mathematics in a school, a group of students conducted a survey.

Q1.

Q2.

Q3.

Date ....   Signed ....

10.2 Statistics – Types of data

1. Using the words

   **NUMERICAL, DATA
   DISCRETE, NOMINAL
   CONTINUOUS, ORDERED
   CATEGORICAL,**

   complete the tree diagram over.

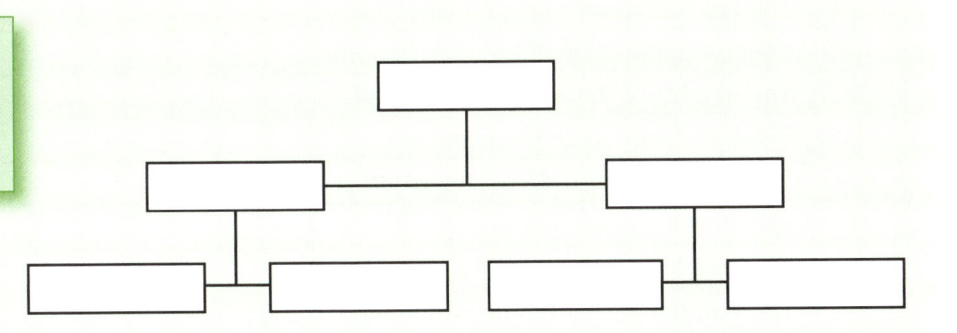

2. Place the letter representing the appropriate definition beside the correct title in the list below.
   [Read the list carefully first]

			Letter
A:	Data that is collected in groups	Data	
B:	Data collected from outside sources	Primary data	
C:	Data that is collected in ordered groups	Secondary data	
D:	Information collected by experiment or in response to a question	Discrete numerical data	
E:	Data collected by the person going to use it	Continuous numerical data	
F:	Data that can be measured on some scale	Nominal categorical data	
G:	Data that can be counted	Ordered categorical data	

3. The following is a list of examples of different types or forms of data. Place the letter representing the appropriate example beside the correct title in the list below. [Read the list carefully first]

			Letter
A:	The number of cars in the school carpark	Data	
B:	Counting the number of cars in the school carpark	Primary data	
C:	The weights of students in your class	Secondary data	
D:	Looking at records to see how many babies were born each day in May	Discrete numerical data	
E:	Favourite music group	Continuous numerical data	
F:	Niall bought a 2-door car for €1000	Nominal categorical data	
G:	Premier division, Championship division etc	Ordered categorical data	

Date .... Signed ....

4. State whether the following data is Discrete/Continuous/Categorical.

A:	The number of players on a team.	
B:	The number of doors on a car.	
C:	The types of music played on the radio.	
D:	The temperature of different classrooms.	
E:	The heights of students in your class.	
F:	The time taken to do this exercise.	
G:	The types of fruit sold in a supermarket.	
H:	The cost of a pair of jeans.	
I:	The area of the classroom floor.	
J:	The number of children born in Ireland in 2005.	
K:	Shoe sizes of students in your class.	
L:	The lengths of feet of students in your class.	
M:	The amount (volume) of cola in bottles.	
N:	The cost of fruit.	
O:	The favorite colours of students in your class.	
P:	The colour of eys of students in first-year.	
Q:	Wind speeds measured at an airport.	
R:	Types of cars sold by a car dealer.	
S:	Grades awarded in the Leaving Certificate.	

5. Write two questions each of which would produce
   (a) Discrete
   (b) Continuous
   (c) Categorical data
      (not already mentioned above)

(a) Discrete	(i)
	(ii)
(b) Continuous	(i)
	(ii)
(c) Categorical	(i)
	(ii)

Date .... Signed ....

10.3 Statistics – Graphical methods

Write the terms –
stem and leaf plot,
line plot, bar-chart,
under the appropriate diagram.

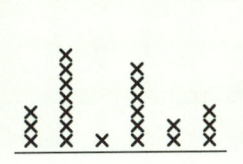

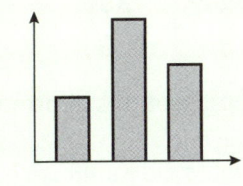

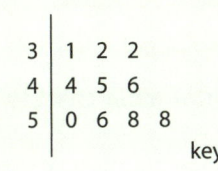

1.

Colour of car	Silver	Red	White	Blue	Black
Number of cars	10	2	3	4	5

   (a) Draw a bar chart of this information.

   (b) How many cars were in the carpark?

   (c) Which is the least popular car colour?

   (d) What fraction of cars are silver?

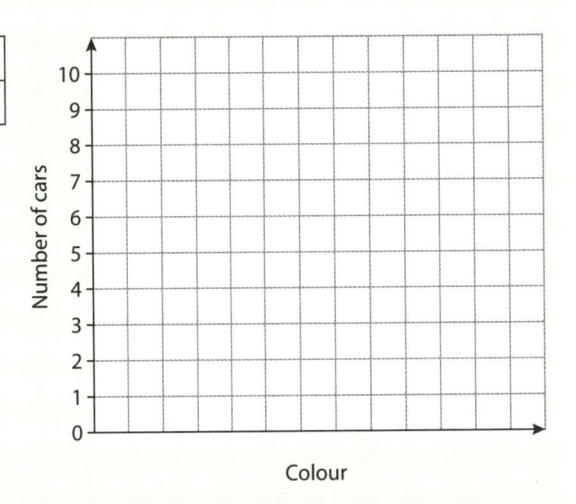

2. Two classes of students were surveyed on subject choices for 5th year. Using the bar chart complete the following table.

	Physics	Biology	Chemistry	Geography	Totals
Class 1	6				
Class 2		6	10		24
Totals					

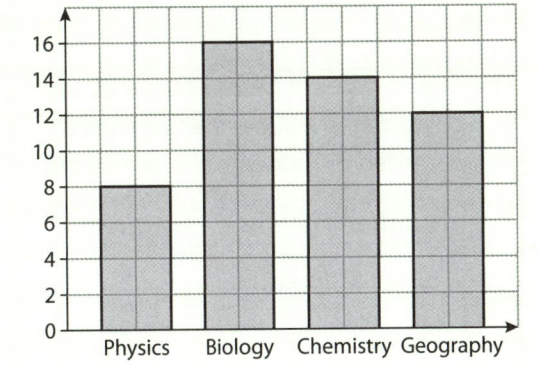

   (a) How many students were surveyed?

   (b) How many students were in class 1?

   (c) What fraction of students selected (i) Physics   (ii) Chemistry

3. This table gives the data on shoe sizes collected in a class.

Shoe size	4	5	6	7	8
Number of students	4	8	10	6	2

   (a) Draw a bar chart of this data.

   (b) How many students were in the class?

   (c) What fraction of the class did not wear size 6?

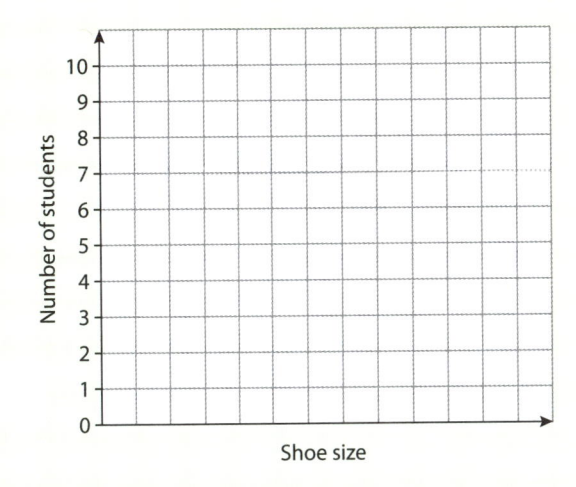

Date .... Signed ....

4. The list below gives the number of votes five students got to be class rep.

Zak	Katie	Jodey	Ross	Kamil
4	10	6	3	7

(a) Draw a bar chart to represent this information.

(b) What fraction of the votes did Kamil get?

(c) What percentage of the votes did Jody get?   =   %

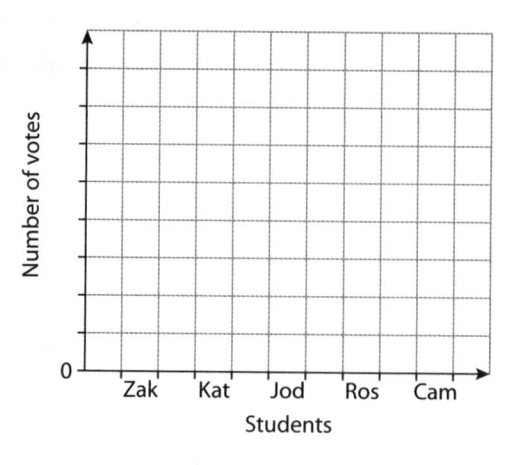

5. The colour of eyes of all the first years in a school is given below. Use a horizontal bar chart to represent this data.

Colour	Frequency
Blue	25
Brown	30
Grey	10
Hazel	15

What fraction of students did not have Blue eyes?

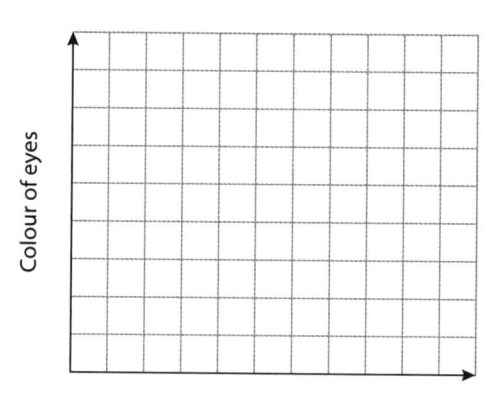

6. The number of items bought by each customer in a supermarket were recorded as follows.

Number of items	Frequency
1–5	9
6–10	8
11–15	7
16–20	8
21–25	6
26–30	4

Draw a bar chart of this information.

7. This bar chart shows the number of animals visiting the vet at the weekend.

(a) How many animals in total visited the vet?

(b) What percentage were <u>not</u> cats or dogs?

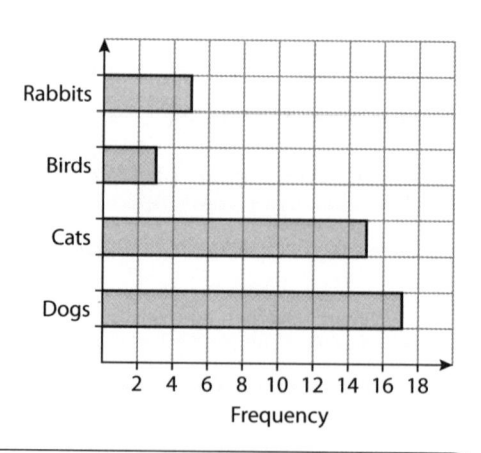

Date ....   Signed ....

8. This line plot indicates the number of brothers or sisters each student has in a first year class.

   (a) How many students were in the class?

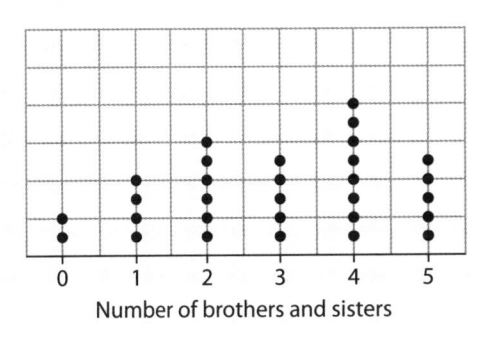

   (b) How many students had three or more brothers or sisters?

   (c) How many "only-children" were in this class?

   (d) What percentage of students had 1, 2 or 3 brothers or sisters?   =   %

9. Draw a line plot of the marks obtained by a class of maths students.

Mark	10	20	30	40	50
Number of students	1	2	5	12	10

   (a) What fraction of students got full marks?

   (b) If 30 marks or more were needed to pass, what percentage of students failed?

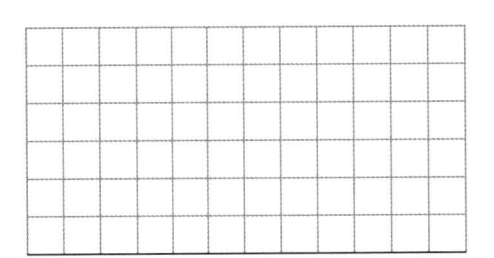

10. Draw a line plot of the number of goals scored per team in a league.

Goals	0	1	2	3	4	5
Number of teams	3	7	4	8	2	1

   (a) How many teams were in the league?

   (b) What fraction of the league scored 2 goals or more?

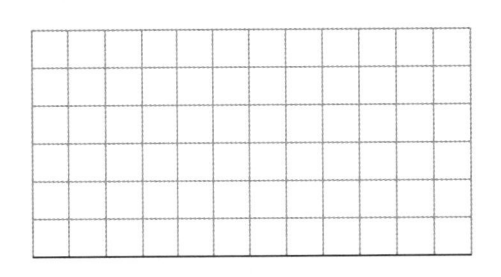

   (c) What percentage of the league scored less than 2 goals?

11. A five question quiz was given to a number of first year students.

   (a) How many girls were in the quiz?

   (b) What fraction of the boys get full marks in the quiz?

   (c) Who performed better in the quiz, boys or girls?

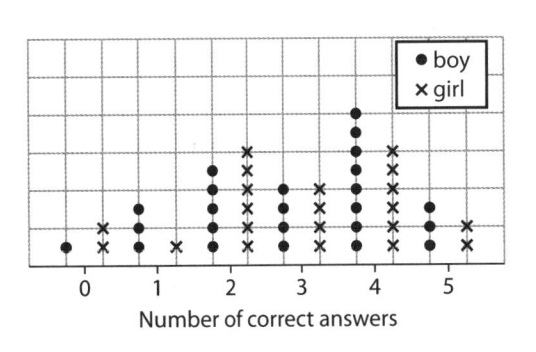

Date ....   Signed ....

12. Represent the following data as a stem and leaf plot.

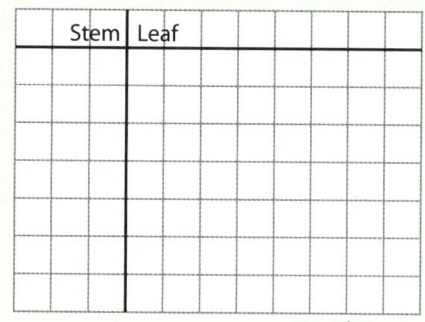

30, 32, 56, 47, 41, 35, 59,
60, 34, 50, 52, 44, 46, 52,
43, 48

Stem	Leaf

Key 3|2 = 32

13. Represent the following data as a stem and leaf plot.

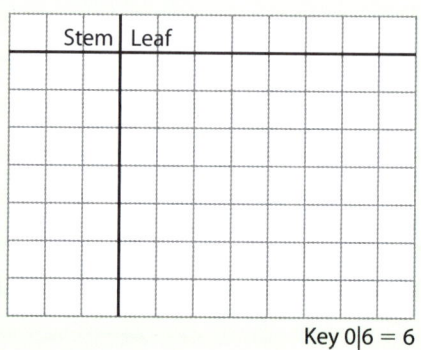

29, 6, 12, 14, 33, 11, 12,
15, 20, 27, 15, 30, 24, 26,
18, 22, 8, 18, 26, 29, 23

Stem	Leaf

Key 0|6 = 6

14. Represent the following data as a stem and leaf plot.

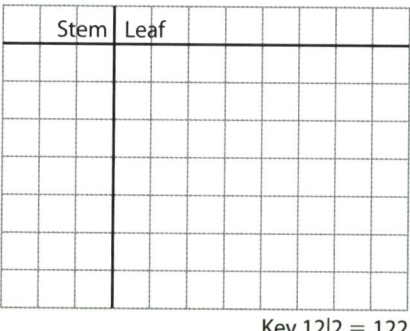

149, 118, 122, 152, 146, 137, 133,
128, 158, 145, 139, 134, 128, 145,
136, 130, 125, 148, 147, 149, 138,
132, 108, 154, 148

(a) If these numbers represent the heights in cm of students in a class, how many students were over 120 cm tall?

(b) What fraction of students were less than 120 cm tall?

Stem	Leaf

Key 12|2 = 122

15. This stem and leaf plot shows the number of text messages sent or received by students in a class per week.

(a) What was the least number of tests?

(b) What was the largest number of tests?

(c) How many students sent or received an even number of text messages?

(d) What fraction of students sent or received less than 30 messages?

(e) What fraction of students sent or received at least 35 messages?

Stem	Leaf
0	6 8 8 9
1	2 4 4 7 8
2	1 2 4 6
3	0 1 2 3 5 8 8
4	2 6 9
5	0 0 4 4 7
6	3 7 9

Key 6|3 = 63

Date .... Signed ....

11.1 Counting

In statistics to tally means to count or total separate parts of a set of data.

This is a tally of the blue, black, white or silver cars passing the gates of a school in 5 minutes.

Colour of car	Tally	Frequency
Blue	IIII	4
Black	HHT HHT I	11
White	HHT II	7
Silver	HHT HHT HHT III	18

1. A dice is rolled 60 times. Make a tally of the numbers rolled and find the total or frequency of each number.

Number on die	Tally	Frequency
1		
2		
3		
4		
5		
6		

Based on your tally is this a fair dice?

Explain:

Based on your tally which number is (a) most likely to turn up

(b) least likely to turn up?

2. Using the following sentence do a tally of the vowels used.

"The square of the length of the hypotenuse of a right-angled triangle is equal to the sum of the squares of the lengths of the other two sides."

Vowel	Tally	Frequency
a		
e		
i		
o		
u		

Based on your tally which vowel would appear to be

(a) the most common

(b) the least common?

Date .... Signed ....

3. Using the following sentence do a tally of the vowels used and compare it to a tally for the letters p, q, r, s and t.

   "When you question a random sample you should get a result that is very similar to the one you would get if you questioned all the members of the group."

   Based on your tally which vowel would appear to be

   (a) the most common

   (b) the least common?

Letter	Tally	Frequency
a		
e		
i		
o		
u		
p		
q		
r		
s		
t		

Based on this tally, which of these consonants is the most common

Give a reason for the difference in frequency between vowels and consonants based on this random sample.

4. Using this tally chart for the blue, red, silver and white cars parked in a car park find

   (a) the total (frequency) of each colour

   (b) the fraction of (i) blue cars

   (ii) white cars

Colour of car	Tally	Frequency
Blue	|||| |||| ||||	
Red	|||| ||	
Silver	|||| |||| |||| |||| |||| |||	
White	|||| ||||	
	Total	

5. Two classes of students were asked to name their favourite sport from a list of football, tennis, swimming and basketball.

   Complete the frequency column of the tally chart.

   (a) What was the total number of students in the two classes?

   (b) What percentage of students preferred tennis?

   (c) What was the difference in the percentage between those who preferred tennis to those who preferred football?

Sport	Tally	Frequency
Football	|||| |||| |||| |||| ||||	
Tennis	|||| ||||	
Swimming	||||	
Basketball	|||| ||||		
	Total	

6. A class of 30 students were asked to record the name of one flower each. DAFFODIL, DAISY, ROSE and TULIP were the only flowers recorded.

   Complete the frequency table shown if 50% of them wrote ROSE, 20% of them wrote TULIP and the least number said DAISY.

   What fraction of the class voted for the DAFFODIL?

Flower	Tally	Frequency
		6
		4
		15
		5
	Total	

Date .... Signed ....

11.2 The Fundamental Principle of Counting

Remember:
If there are m ways of doing one thing and n ways of doing another then there are $m \times n$ ways of doing both.

If we can pick from 2 different shapes each with 3 different colours we have a total of

$2 \times 3 = 6$ choices

1. How many different tiles can be chosen if each tile can come in 4 different sizes each size having 3 different patterns?   =

2. At dinner in a restaurant I pick one starter, one main course and one dessert. If the menu offers a choice of 3 starters, 5 main courses and 4 desserts

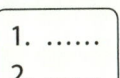

   Starter Mains Dessert

   How many meal choices have I altogether?

   =

3. At student must pick one subject from each of the following bands

   Band A
   - Physics
   - Chemistry
   - Biology

   Band B
   - Geography
   - History
   - Business Studies

   Band C
   - French
   - German
   - Spanish

   How many choices has she altogether?

   =

4. How many different doors are possible?
   - 3 different designs of door
   - 5 different colours
   - 3 different choices of letterbox

   =

5. One box contains discs 0, 1, 2, 3, 4, 5, 6, 7, 8, 9 and a second box contains discs 1, 4, 5, 7, 9.
   How many different numbers can be formed if I can only pick one number from each box?

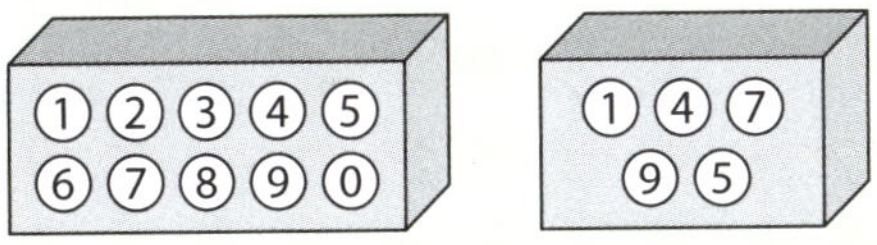

   =

   What is the smallest number and the largest number possible from this experiment?

   smallest =
   largest =

6. 2, 4, 6, 8, 0   a, e, i, o, u   1, 3, 5, 7, 9

   A code is made by picking a number from 0, 2, 4, 6, 8, followed by a vowel a, e, i, o, u, followed by a number 1, 3, 5, 7, 9.
   How many codes are possible?   =

7. A lock has 3 rings each containing the digits 0 to 9.
   How many combinations are possible?   =

Date ....   Signed ....

11.3 Probability

0 0.1 0.2 0.3 0.4 0.5 0.6 0.7 0.8 0.9 1
(impossible)   (unlikely)   (50-50)   (likely)   (certain)

1. Use one of the terms, impossible, unlikely, 50-50, likely, certain for each of the following.

	Probability
1. The sun is going to shine tomorrow.	
2. It is going to rain some day next week.	
3. That you pick a black card at random from a deck of cards.	
4. That you pick a 2 of diamonds at random from a deck of cards.	
5. That you win the LOTTO.	
6. That a tossed coin will show a HEAD.	
7. That prices will rise in the next two years.	
8. That five will divide into four evenly.	
9. That the host nation will take part in the next football World Cup.	
10. That oil will run out in the next 20 years.	

2. List the NUMBER of outcomes possible in each of the following experiments.

Number of outcomes

(a) Rolling a dice (a) _____

(b) Tossing a coin (b) _____

(c) Picking one card from a normal pack of cards (c) _____

(d) Picking one letter of the alphabet (d) _____

(e) Picking a vowel (e) _____

(f) Picking a consonant (f) _____

(g) Rolling two dice (g) _____

(h) Tossing two coins (h) _____

(i) Rolling a dice and tossing a coin (i) _____

(j) Picking a diamond from a normal pack of cards (j) _____

Date ....   Signed ....

3. A box contains 10 discs numbered 0 to 9.
A disc is chosen at random.
Giving your answer as a fraction, find each of the following probabilities.

(a) The probability of picking an even number.   P(even) = $\frac{4}{10}$

(b) The probability of picking an odd number.   P(odd) =

Remember:
0 is neither even or odd.

(c) The probability of picking a 5.   P(5) =

(d) The probability of picking a multiple of 3.   P(×3) =

(e) The probability of picking a number less than 5.   P(<5) =

(f) The probability of picking a number greater than or equal to 7.   P(≥7) =

4. A prize is won if a coloured square is revealed on a scratch card.
Find the probability of winning a prize on each of the following scratch cards.

A   B   C   D

P(A) =   P(B) =   P(C) =

P(D) =

5. There are 10 girls and 14 boys in a class.
A student rep is chosen at random by placing all the names into a box and drawing out one name.

(a) How many possible outcomes are there?   Number of outcomes =

(b) What is the probability that a boy is chosen?   P(boy) =

(c) Anna was class rep last year.
What is the probability that she will be chosen again this year?   Prob. (Anna) =

6. A bag contains 2 Red, 3 Blue and 3 Green counters.
A counter is chosen at random.
Find, as a fraction, the probability of

(a) a red counter =   (b) a blue counter =

(c) a green counter =   (d) a red *or* a blue counter =

Date ....   Signed ....

7. A bag contains ten counters, five blue, three red and two yellow.
One counter is chosen at random.
Write as a fraction the probability of

(a) picking a red counter   P(red) =

(b) picking a yellow counter   P(yellow) =

(c) picking either a blue or a yellow counter   P(blue or yellow) =

(d) *not* picking a yellow counter   P(not yellow) =

(e) *not* picking either a blue or a red counter   P(not blue or red) =

8. What is the probability that the spinner will land on

(a) yellow   P(yellow) =

(b) green   P(green) =

(c) orange   P(orange) =

(d) yellow or green   P(yellow or green) =

(e) not green   P(not green) =   ?

9. A dice is rolled. What is the probability of a

(a) four   P(4) =

(b) six or a five   P(6 or 5) =

(c) even number   P(even) =

(d) a multiple of 2   P(×2) =   ?

10. A box contains counters numbered 0 to 11 in the shape of triangles, squares and circles. Find each of the following probabilities.

(a) P(square) =   , P(circle) =

(b) P(even number) =   , P(odd number) =

(c) P(a circle with an even number) =   , P(2 digit number) =

(d) P(a square with an odd number) =   , P(triangle) =

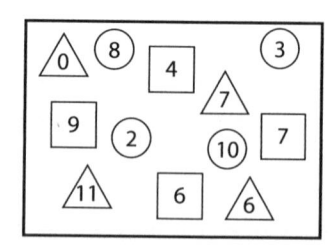

Date ....   Signed ....

11. Roll a dice and toss a coin 60 times. Note the face of the coin and the number on the dice.

Outcome	H1	H2	H3	H4	H5	H6	T1	T2	T3	T4	T5	T6
Tally												
Total												

If both dice and coin were fair (unbiased), what total did you expect for each outcome?

12. Get a square piece of card of side 4 cm.
Draw diagonals across the square and label each segment 1, 2, 3, 4 as shown.
Place a cocktail stick in the centre to make a spinner.
Spin the spinner 40 times and record the outcomes.

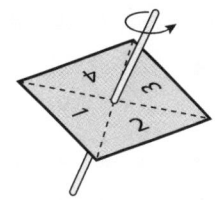

Outcome	Tally	Frequency
1		
2		
3		
4		

What was the expected frequency for this experiment?

13. Repeat the experiment again with the spinner but this time move the cocktail stick 0.5 cm from the centre (along one of the diagonals).

Outcome	Tally	Frequency
1		
2		
3		
4		

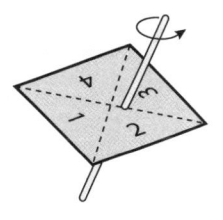

What conclusion can you draw from this experiment?

Date .... Signed ....

12.1 Co-ordinate Geometry

1. Write down the coordinates of each of the labelled points.

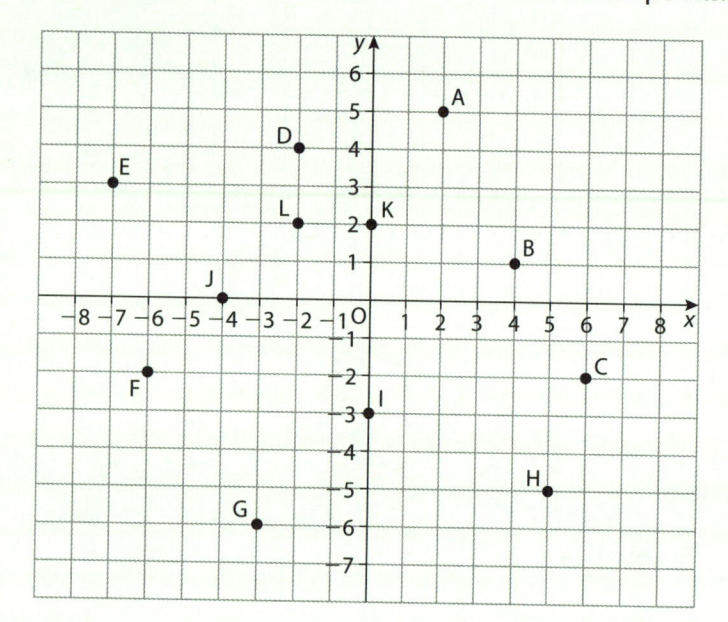

Point	Coordinates
A	(,)
B	(,)
C	(,)
D	(,)
E	(,)
F	(,)
G	(,)
H	(,)
I	(,)
J	(,)
K	(,)
L	(,)

2. Plot each of the following points on the grid provided.
   A (3, 4)
   B (1, −2)
   C (−4, 0)
   D (5, 6)
   E (−3, −3)
   F (0, 5)
   G (0, 0)
   H (−6, 2)
   I (6, 3)
   J (−2, −5)

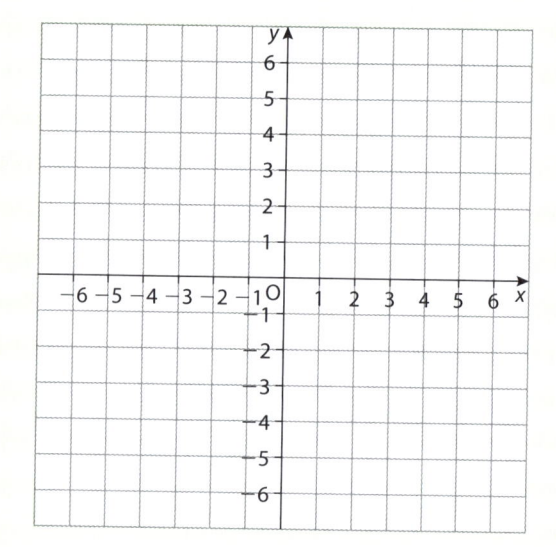

3. Plot the points P(−2, 4), Q(5, 4), R(5, −2) on the grid provided.
   Plot the point S so that PQRS is a rectangle.

   The coordinates of S are (,)

   Find the coordinates of T, the midpoint of PS.

   T = (,)

   Find the coordinates of U so that PQUT is a rectangle.

   U = (,)

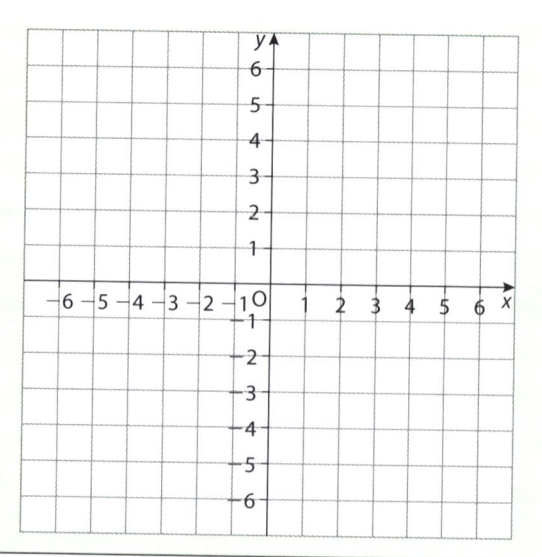

Date .... Signed ....

4. Plot the points (2, 2), (−2, −2) and (−2, 2).

(a) What are the coordinates of a fourth
point that would make a square?   (,)

(b) What are the coordinates of a fourth
point that would make a parallelogram?

(,)   or   (,)

(c) What are the coordinates of a fourth
point that would make a kite shape?

(,)   or   (,)   or   (,)

5. (a) Plot the points A(2, 1) and B(6, 5).
Using the grid, plot the point C, the midpoint of AB.

coordinates of   C = (,)

(b) Plot the points D(−4, −2) and E(0, 4).
Plot the point F the midpoint of DE.

coordinates of   F = (,)

(c) Draw a horizontal line(k) through F.
Name 3 points on k.

_____ , _____ , _____

(d) Draw a vertical line(k) through F.
Name 3 points on k.

_____ , _____ , _____

Remember:

vertical | horizontal

6. Plot the points P(0, 5), Q(6, 6), R(8, 1), S(2, 0)
and join them in the order PQRS.

(a) Write down the coordinates of the
midpoint of [PR].   (,)

(b) Write down the coordinates of the
midpoint of [QS].   (,)

(c) (i) Draw the diagonals of PQRS.
(ii) What do you notice about the diagonals?

Date ....   Signed ....

7. On the grid provided, plot the sets of points

A = (−2, 3), (−1, 2½), (0, 2), (1, 3/2), (2, 1), (3, ½).

B = (−2, 6), (−1, 4), (0, 2), (1, 0), (2, −2), (3, −4).

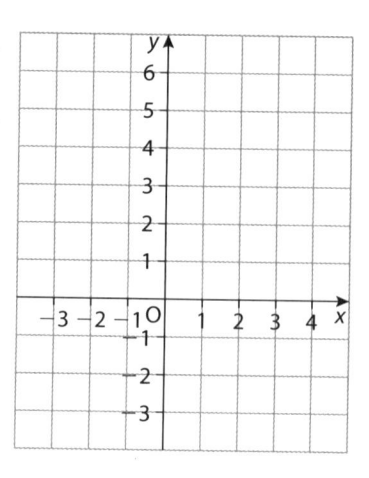

(i) What do you notice about the set of points A?

(ii) What do you notice about the set of points B?

(iii) Find the point A ∩ B =   ,

8. Continue the pattern in each of the following sets of points and hence write down the next three points.

A: (x, y)	B: (x, y)	C: (x, y)	D: (x, y)
(0, 3)	(0, −1)	(0, 2)	(0, −2)
(1, 4)	(1, 1)	(1, 5)	(1, −1)
(2, 5)	(2, 3)	(2, 8)	(2, 0)
(3, 6)	(3, 5)	(3, 11)	(3, 1)
(4,)	(,)	(,)	(,)
(5,)	(,)	(,)	(,)
(6,)	(,)	(,)	(,)

Describe in words how to calculate y, given a value of x.

A: _____

B: _____

C: _____

D: _____

Convert each of the word sentences above into equations for y.

A: y =   C: y =

B: y =   D: y =

9. Using the following equations, find a set of coordinates for each.
Plot each set of points on the graph over.

A	B	C
y = x + 4	y = x + 1	y = x − 3
(x, y)	(x, y)	(x, y)
(0,)	(0,)	(0,)
(1,)	(1,)	(1,)
(2,)	(2,)	(2,)
(3,)	(3,)	(3,)
(4,)	(4,)	(4,)
(5,)	(5,)	(5,)

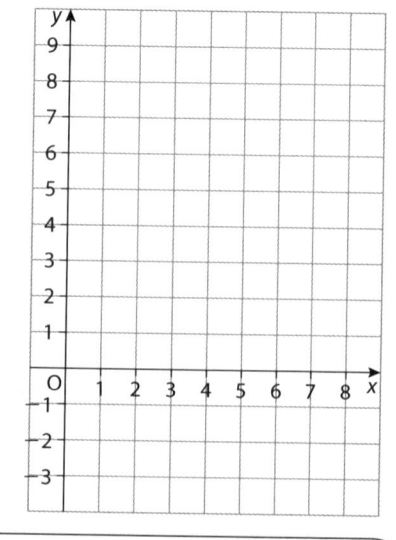

Date ....   Signed ....

12.2 Vertex – Edge – Face

V = Vertices
E = Edges
F = Faces

In each of the following 3–D diagrams, count
  (i) the number of vertices (corners)
  (ii) the number of edges
  (iii) the number of faces.

Then find the value of V − E + F = ?

(a)

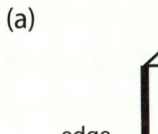

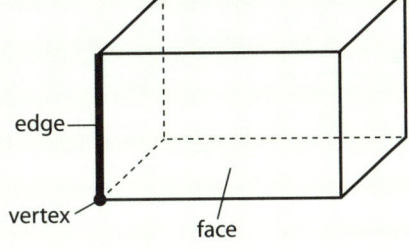

edge
vertex
face

V − E + F
( ) − ( ) + ( ) =

(b)

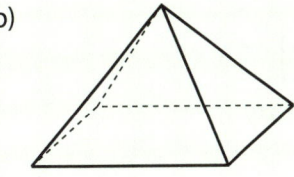

V − E + F
( ) − ( ) + ( ) =

(c)

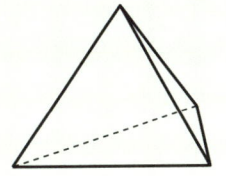

V − E + F
( ) − ( ) + ( ) =

(d)

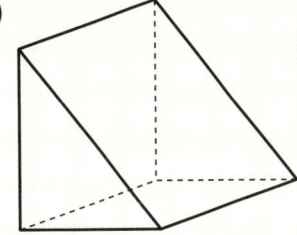

V − E + F
( ) − ( ) + ( ) =

(e)

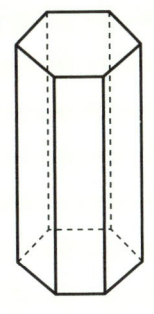

V − E + F
( ) − ( ) + ( ) =

(f)

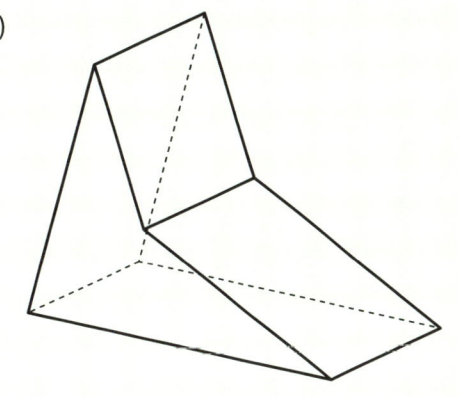

V − E + F
( ) − ( ) + ( ) =

Date .... Signed ....

12.3 Axial Symmetry/Central Symmetry

1. Draw all the lines of symmetry connected with each of the following shapes. Indicate how many lines you found.

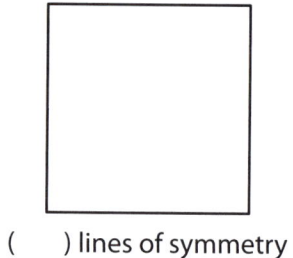

(   ) lines of symmetry

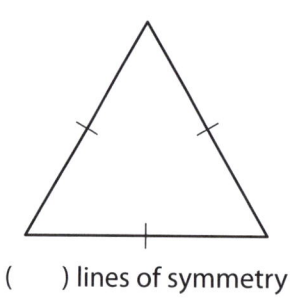

(   ) lines of symmetry

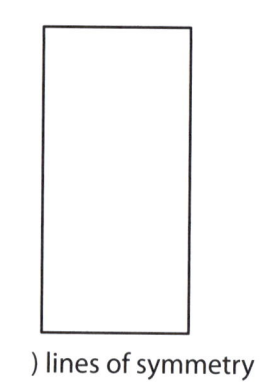

(   ) lines of symmetry

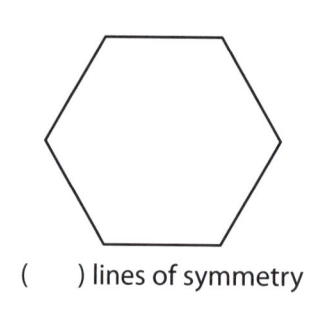

(   ) lines of symmetry

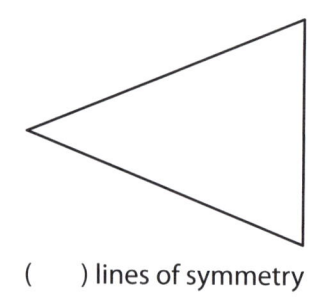

(   ) lines of symmetry

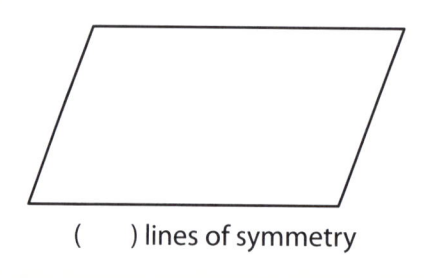

(   ) lines of symmetry

2. Draw an axis of symmetry on each of the following diagrams. (Use a ruler and a coloured pencil.)

(a)

(b)

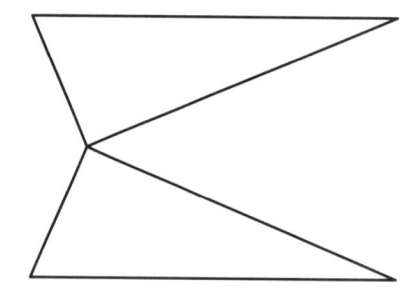

Date ………………………………   Signed ………………………………………………………………

(c)

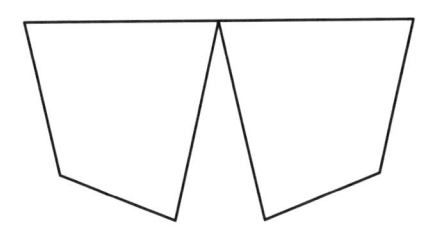

(d)

(c)

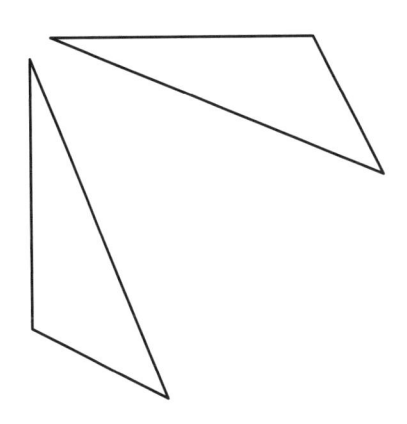

(d)

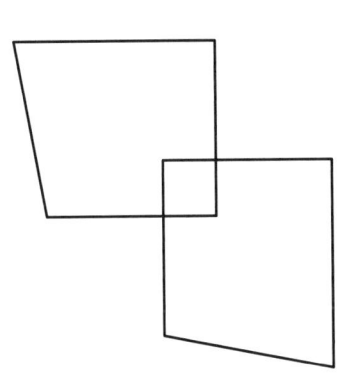

(e)

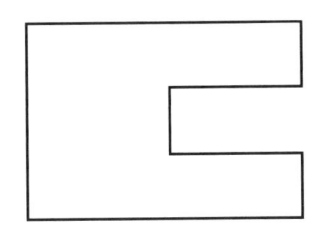

(f)

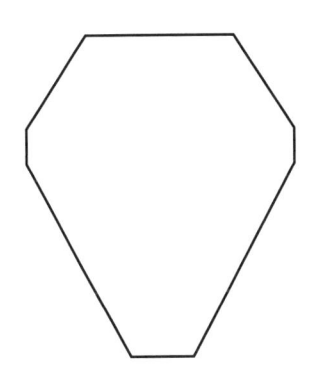

3. Find the image of each of the following in the axis given.

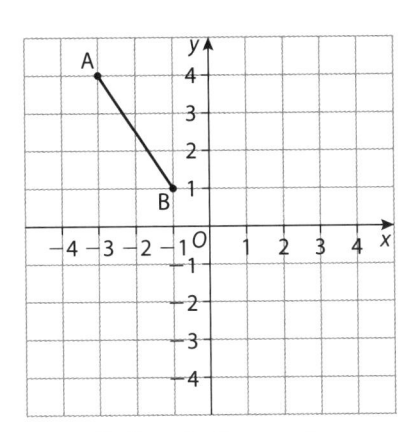

Reflect in the y-axis

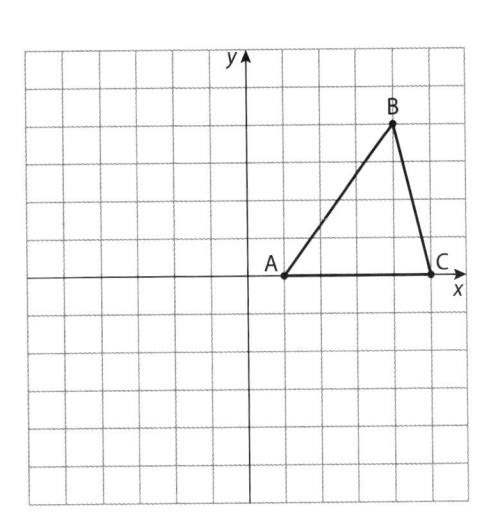

Reflect in the x-axis

Date .... Signed ....

4. Find the image of each of the following sets of points in the axis of symmetry given.

(a)

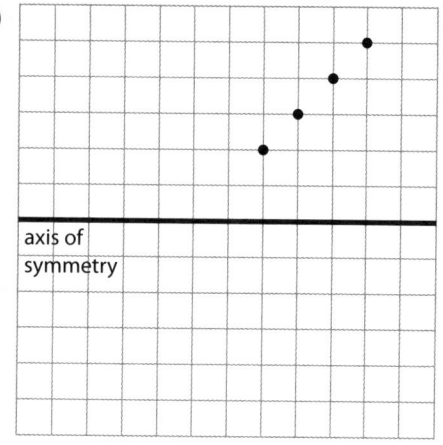

(b)

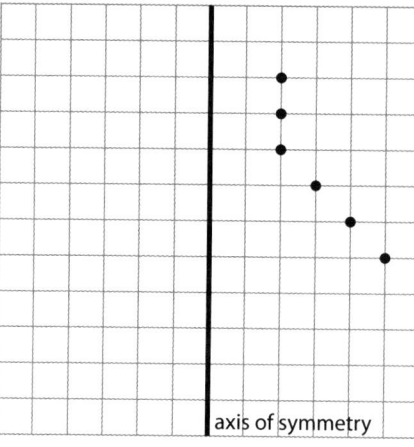

(c)

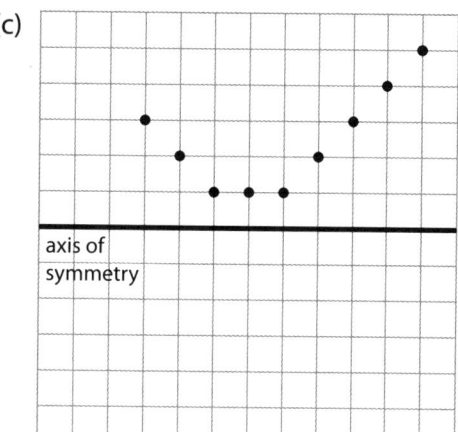

(d)

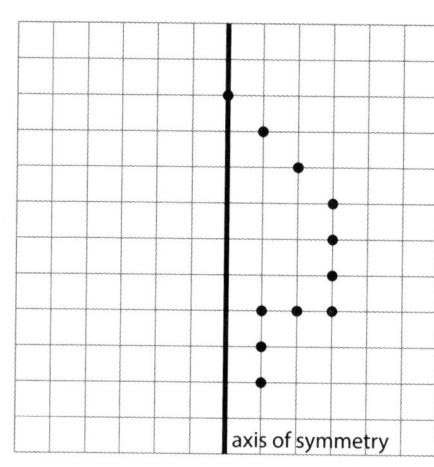

(e)

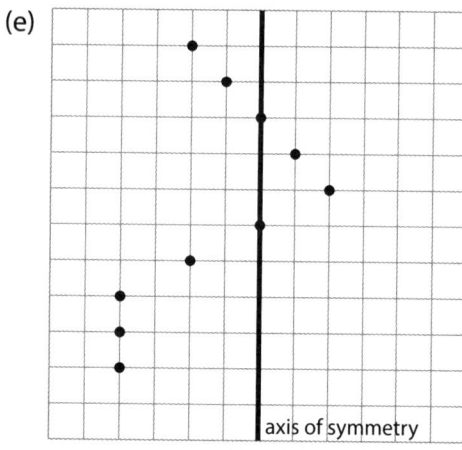

(f)

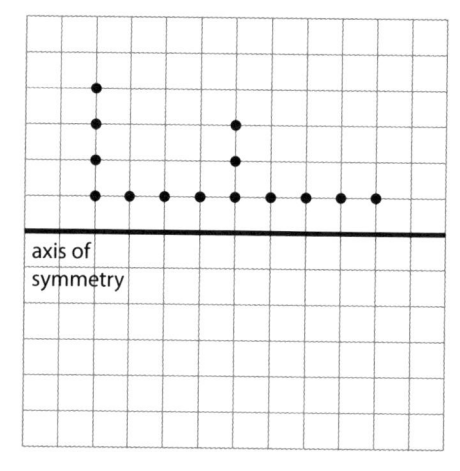

(g)

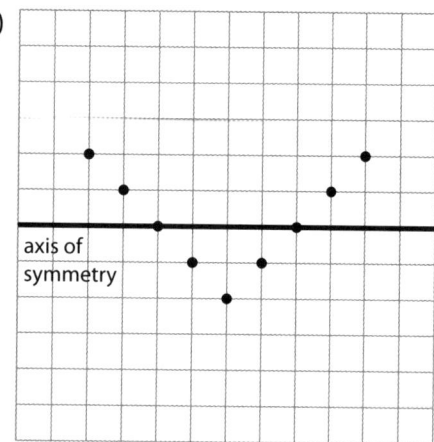

(h)

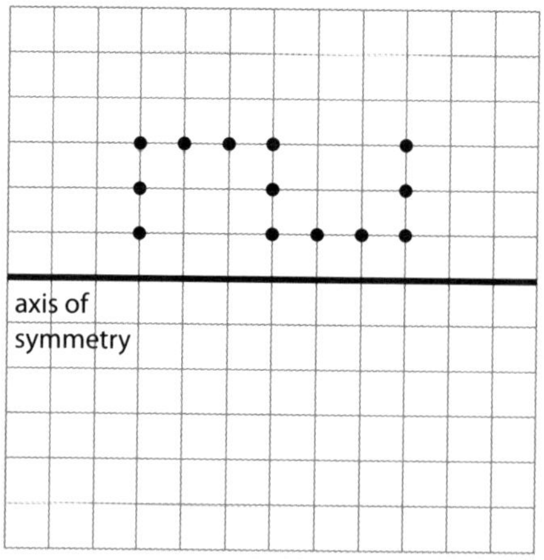

Date .... Signed ....

5. Using the grids provided, find the image of each of the given shapes in the required axis. (Shade in your answer where possible.)

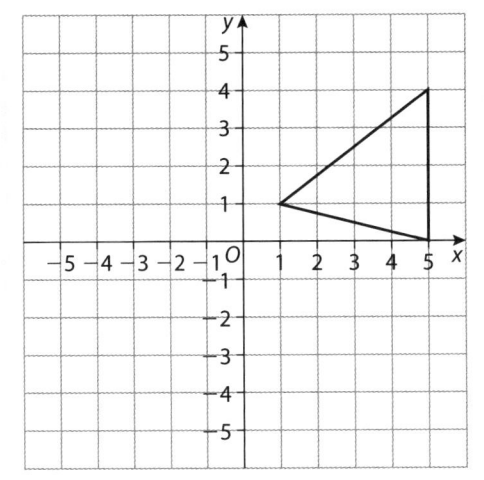

Reflect in the *x*-axis

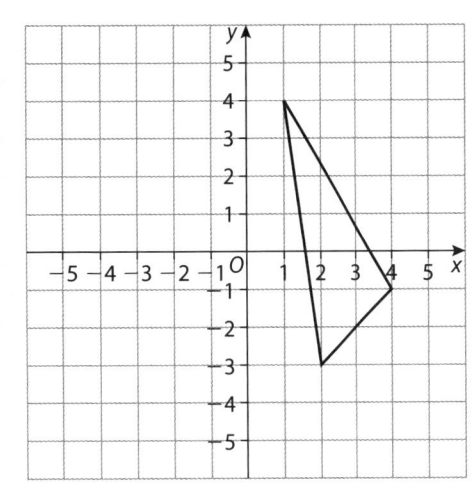

Reflect in the *y*-axis

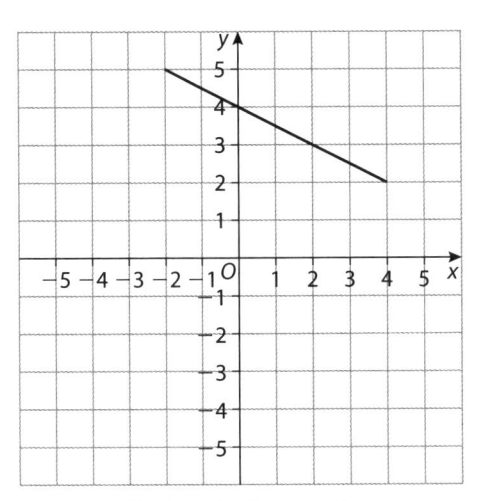

Reflect in the *y*-axis

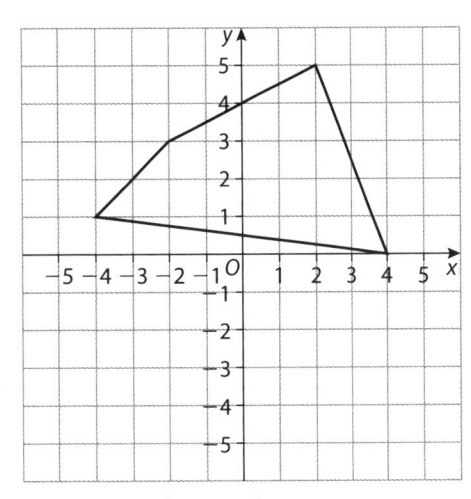

Reflect in the *x*-axis

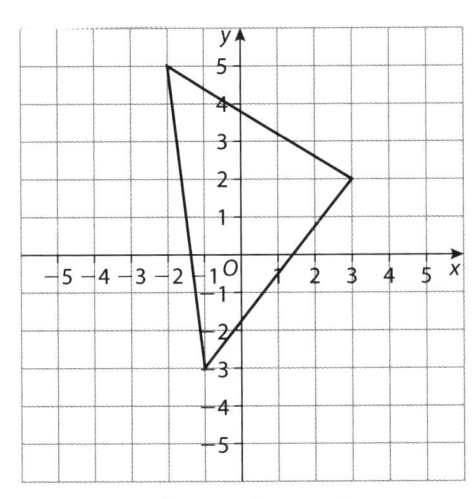

Reflect in the *y*-axis

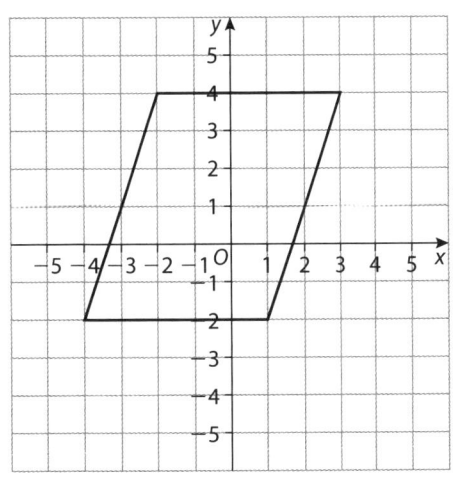

Reflect in the *y*-axis

Date ....   Signed ....

6. Using the grids provided, reflect each shaded shape accurately in the line of symmetry given.

(a) Reflect in the y-axis

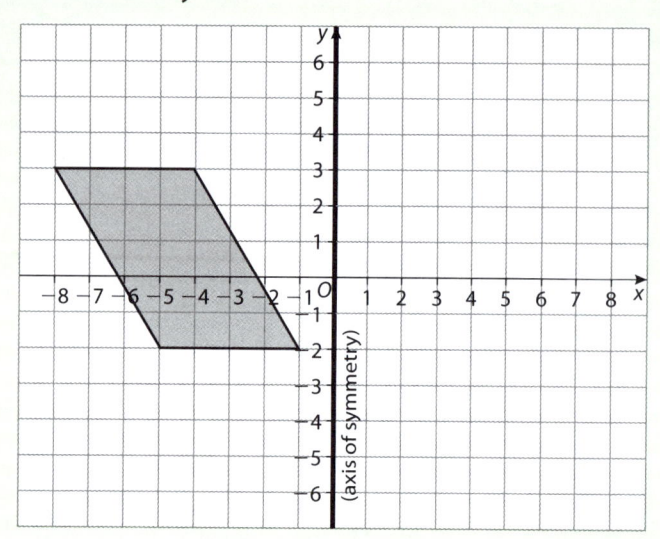

(b) Reflect in the line $x = 2$

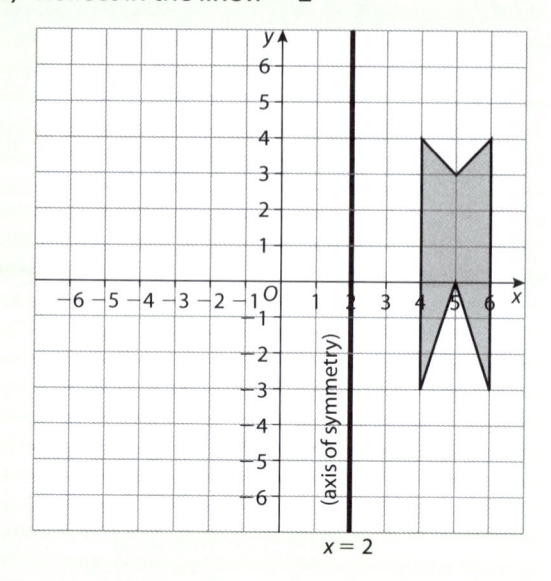

(c) Reflect in the line $x = -2$

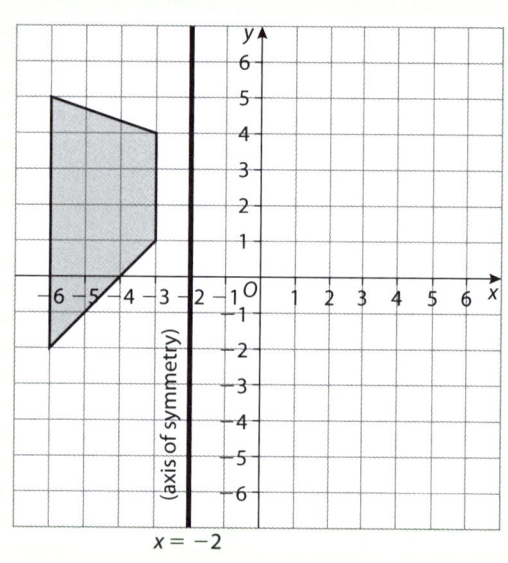

(d) Reflect in the x-axis

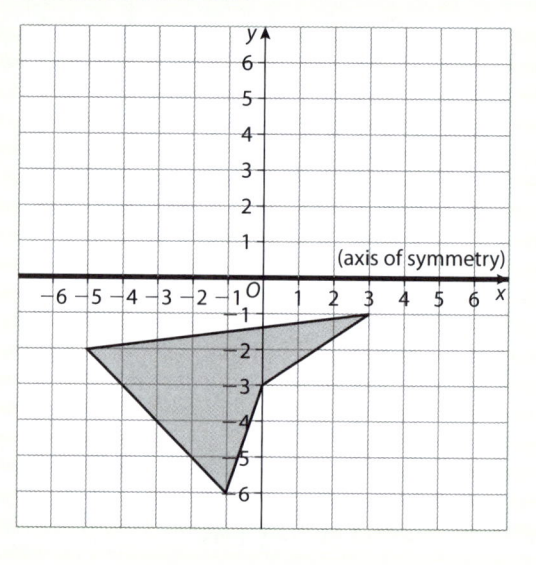

(e) Reflection in the line $x = 1$

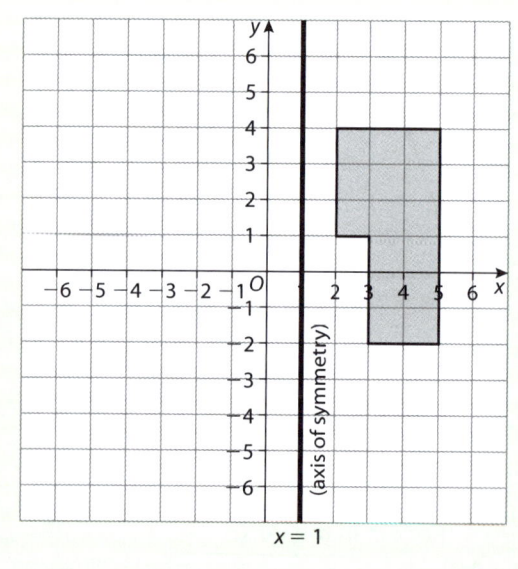

(f) Reflection in the line $y = -2$

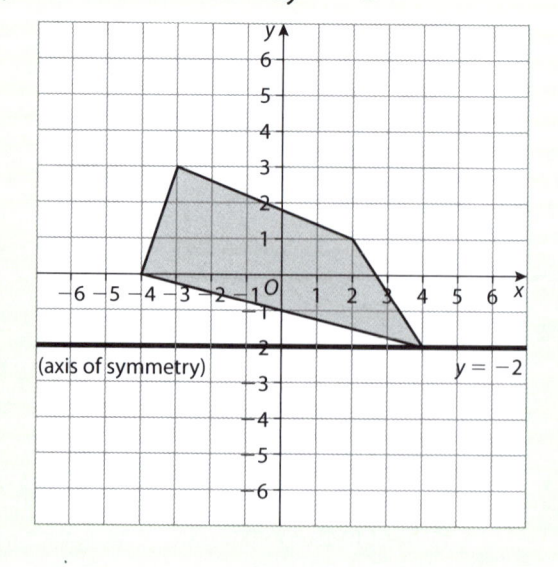

Date .... Signed ....

7. Using the grids provided, reflect each shaped shape accurately in the line of symmetry given.

Reflect in the line $y = 1$

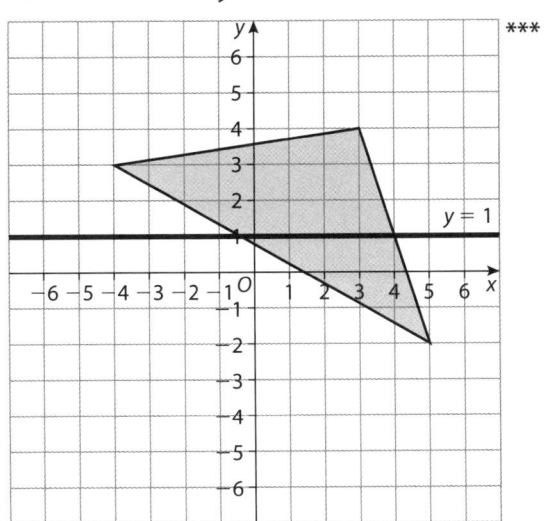

Reflect in the line $x = -2$

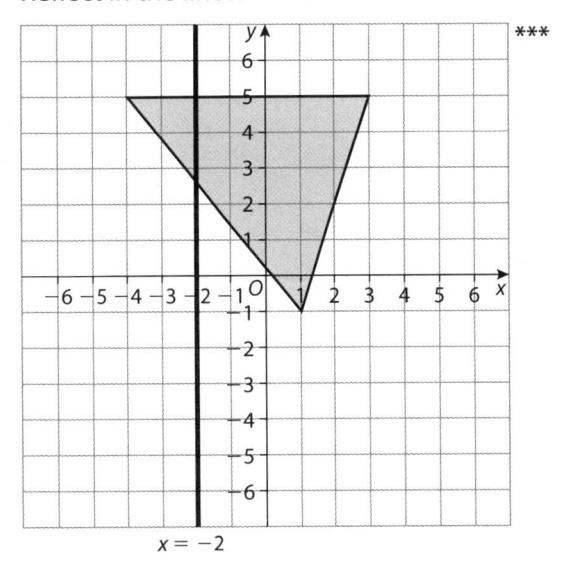

Reflect in the line $y = x$

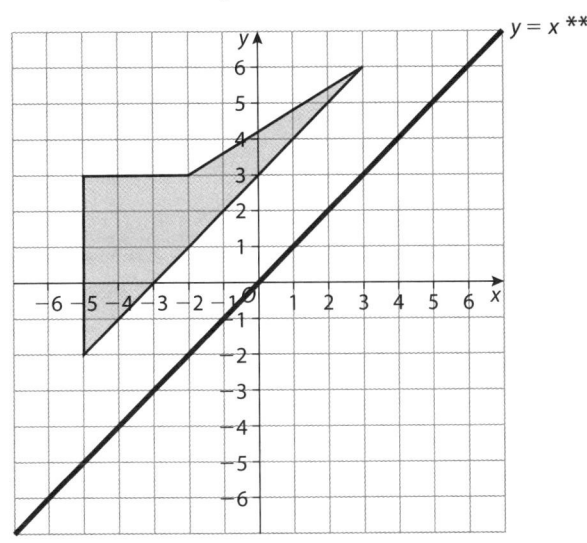

Reflect in the line $y = x$

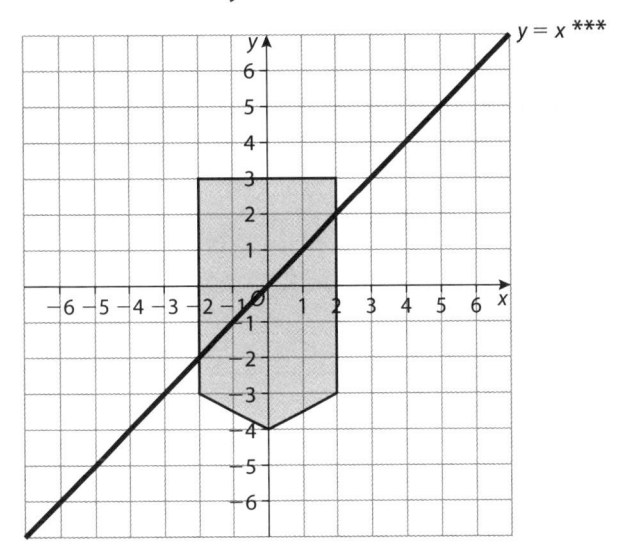

Reflect in the line $y = -x$

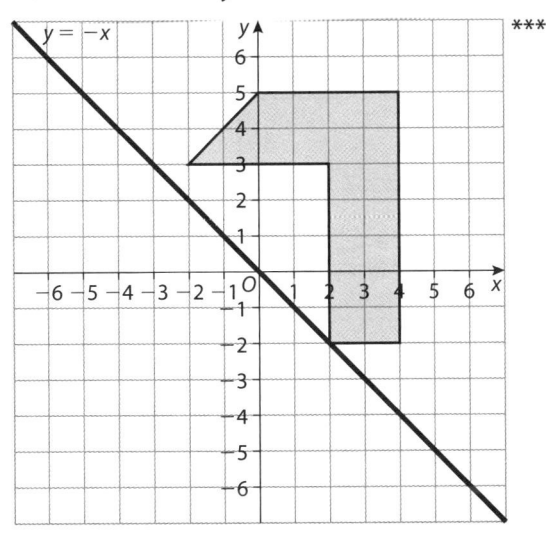

Reflect in the line $y = -x$

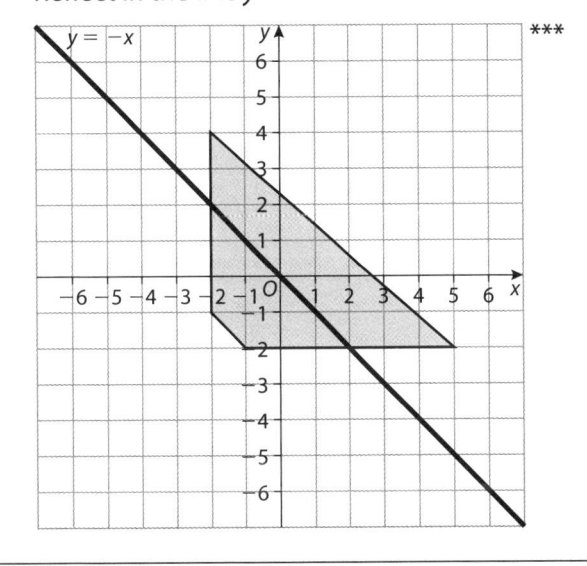

Date .... Signed ....

8. Construct the reflected image of each of the following shapes in the line of symmetry given. Use a set square and ruler.

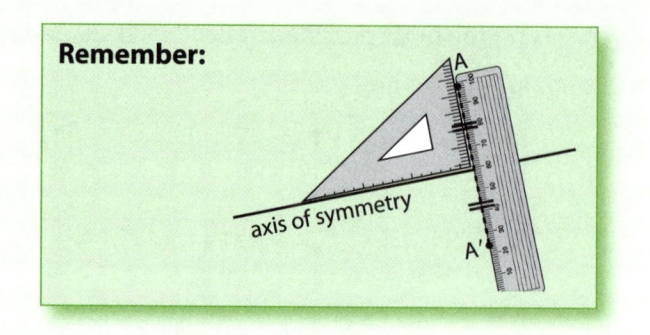

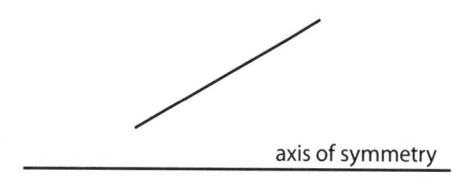

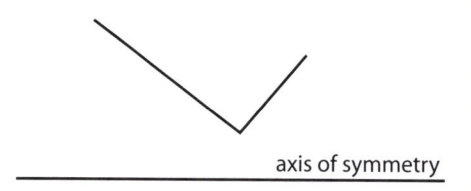

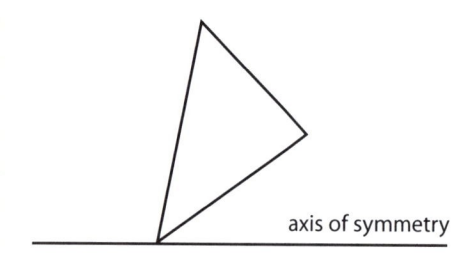

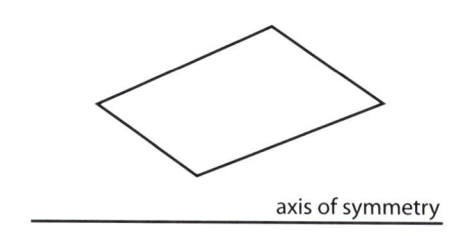

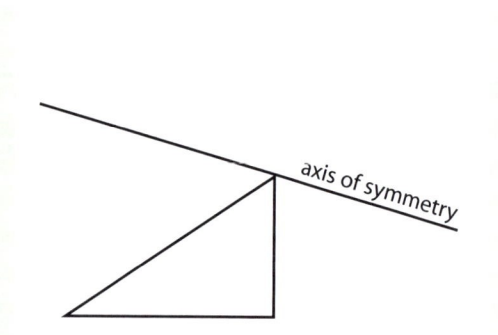

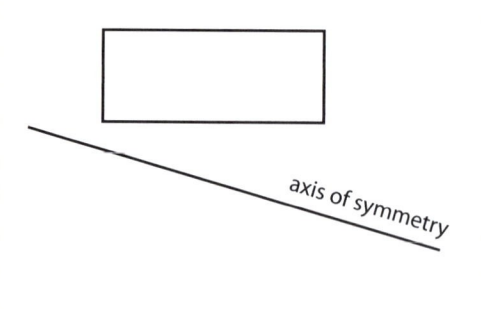

Remember:

axis of symmetry

axis of symmetry

axis of symmetry

axis of symmetry

axis of symmetry

axis of symmetry

Date .... Signed ....

9. Find the image of each shaded shape reflected in the point given.

Remember:

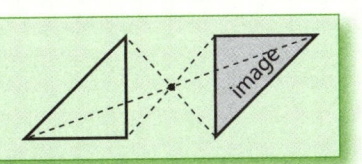

In the point (0, 0)

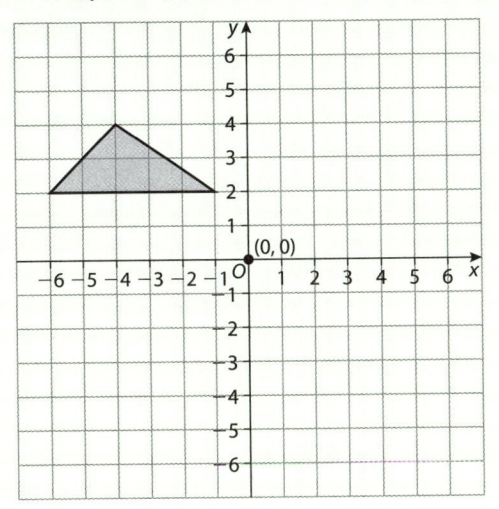

In the point (0, 0)

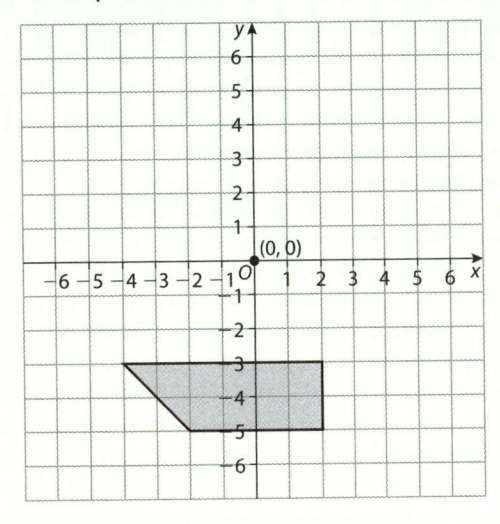

In the point (0, 0)

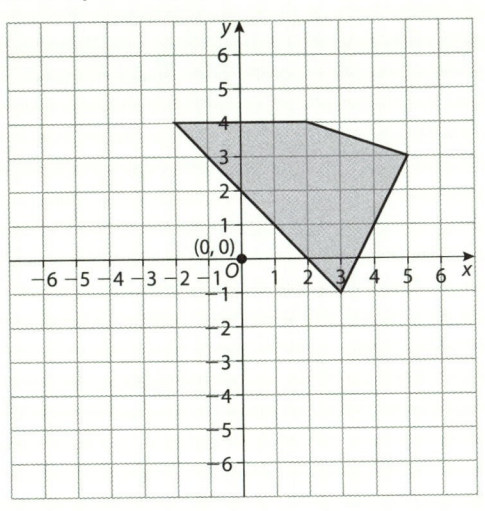

In the point (0, 0)

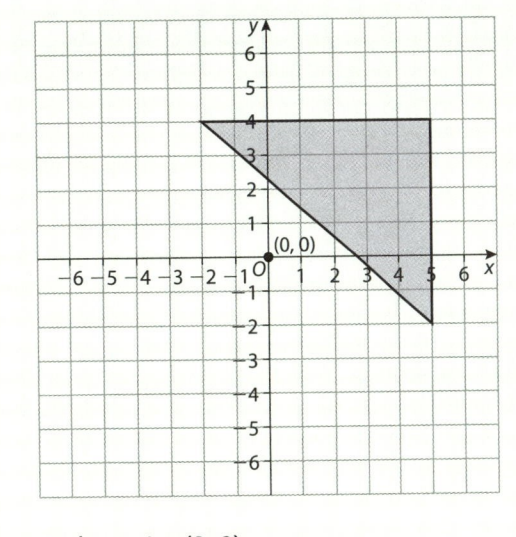

In the point (0, 2)

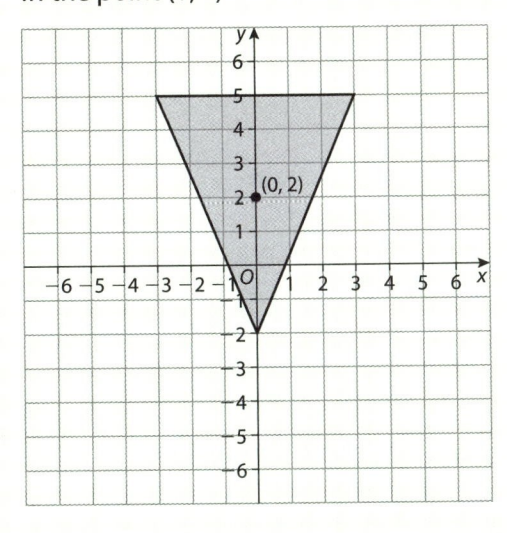

In the point (2, 0)

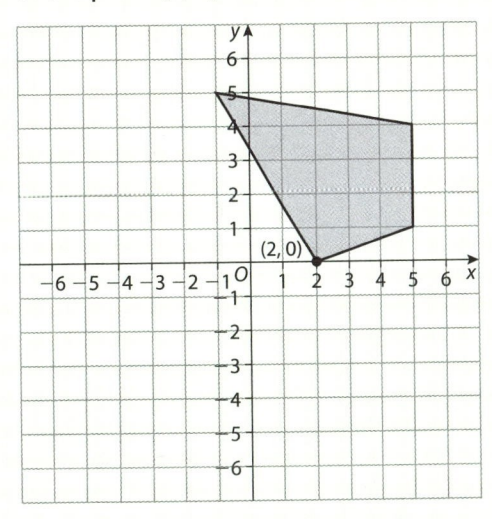

Date .... Signed ....

10. Using a ruler, construct the image of each of the following shapes, in the given point X,

Remember:

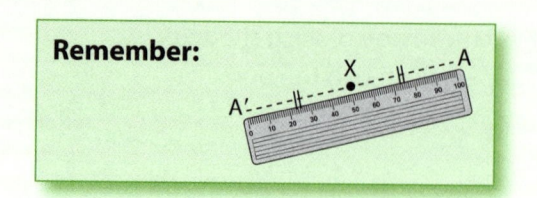

(a)

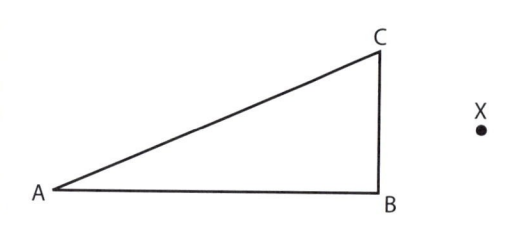

(b)

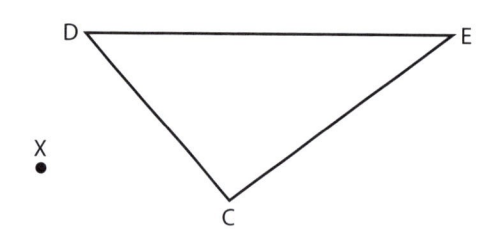

(c)

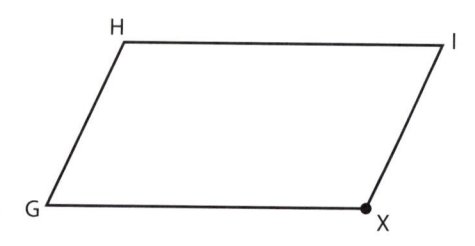

Date ....   Signed ....

(d)

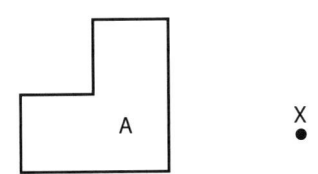

A   •X

(e)

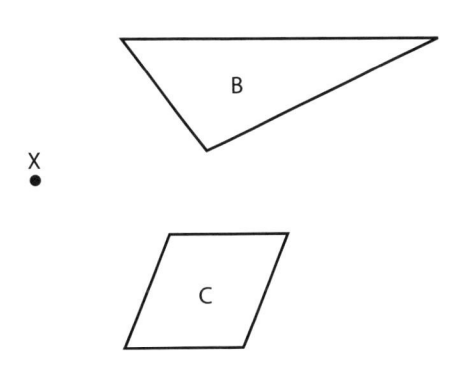

B

•X

C

(f)

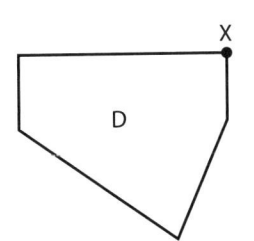

•X
D

Date ....   Signed ....

12.4 Experiments in Reflection

A.

1. Reflect the shape ABC in the line *l*. Label the image A′B′C′.
2. Reflect the shape A′B′C′ in the line *k*. Label the image A″B″C″.
3. Measure the distance AA″, BB″ and CC″ in squares. AA″ =
   BB″ =
   CC″ =
4. Measure the distance *lk* in squares.   *lk* =
5. What conclusions can be drawn from the double reflection?

   1.
   2.

B.

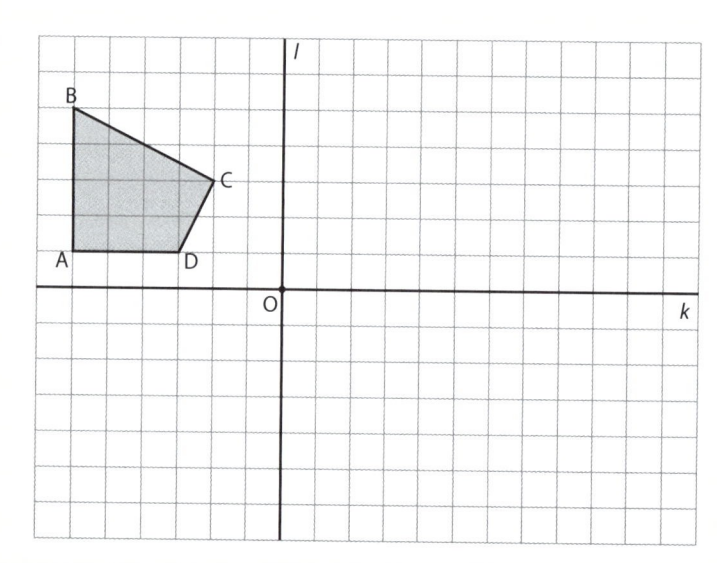

1. Reflect the shape ABCD in the line *l*. Label the image A′B′C′D′.
2. Reflect the shape A′B′C′D′ in the line *k*. Label the image A″B″C″D″.
3. Measure the distance AO and OA″   AO =   OA″ =
   BO and OB″   BO =   OB″ =
   (Use a ruler) CO and OC″   CO =   OC″ =
   DO and OD″.   DO =   OD″ =

4. What conclusion can be drawn from this double reflection?

   Conclusion

Date ....   Signed ....

C. The diagrams below show incomplete mosaic patterns.
Complete each pattern by shading the **4 appropriate tiles** that produce a symmetrical pattern.
When completed, draw the line(s) of symmetry on each diagram.

(i) 2 lines of symmetry

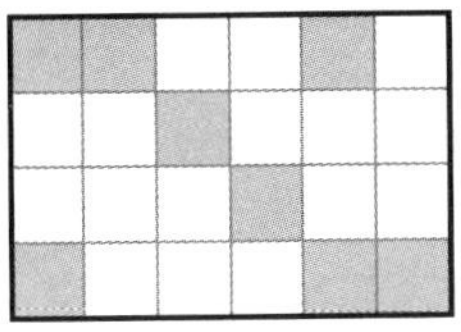

(ii) 1 line of symmetry

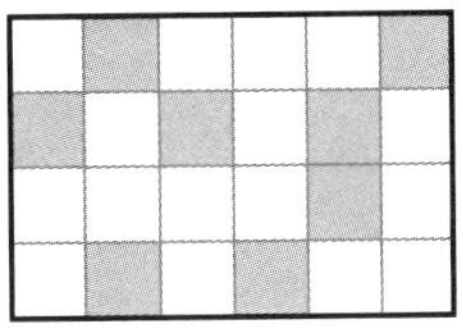

(iii) 1 line of symmetry

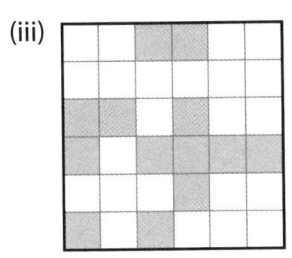

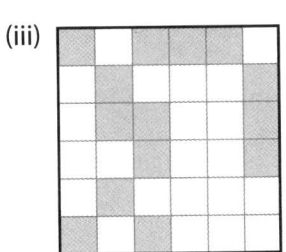

(iii) 1 line of symmetry

D. The letter (upper case) H has two axes of symmetry as shown.

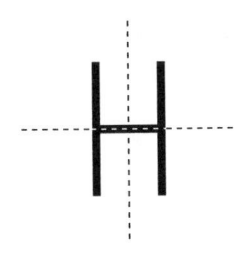

List the other upper case letters of the alphabet that have two axes of symmetry.

E. The letter (upper case) A has one axis of symmetry as shown.

List the other upper case letters of the alphabet that have one axis of symmetry.

F. List the letters of the alphabet (upper case) that have **No** axis of symmetry.

Date .... Signed ....

12.5 Geometry IV

Remember:
when bisecting ...
(a) have a sharp pencil
(b) adjust compass before you start

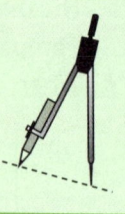

1.

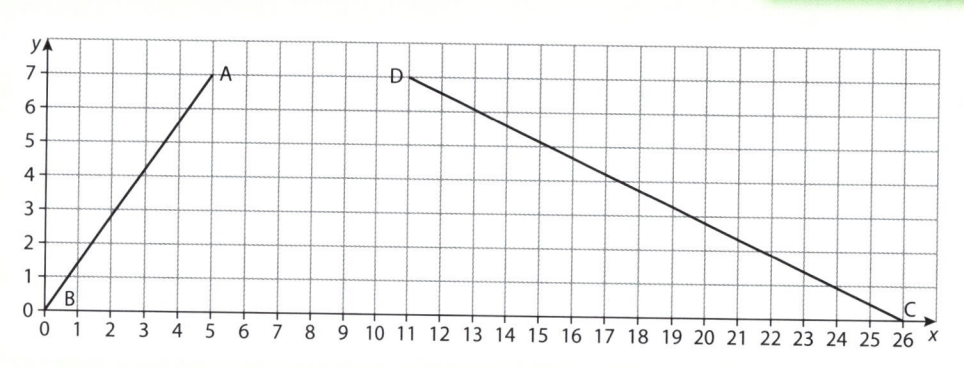

(a) Using a compass and ruler only, bisect ∠ABC and ∠BCD.

(b) Using the grid, find the point of intersection of the bisectors. ,

2. (a) Bisect the angles ∠POR and ∠PRO using only a compass and straight edge.

(b) Using the grid, find the point of intersection of the bisectors.
    ,

(c) Bisect the angle ∠PRS. Call the bisector RT.

(d) Using a protractor measure the angle ∠TRS.

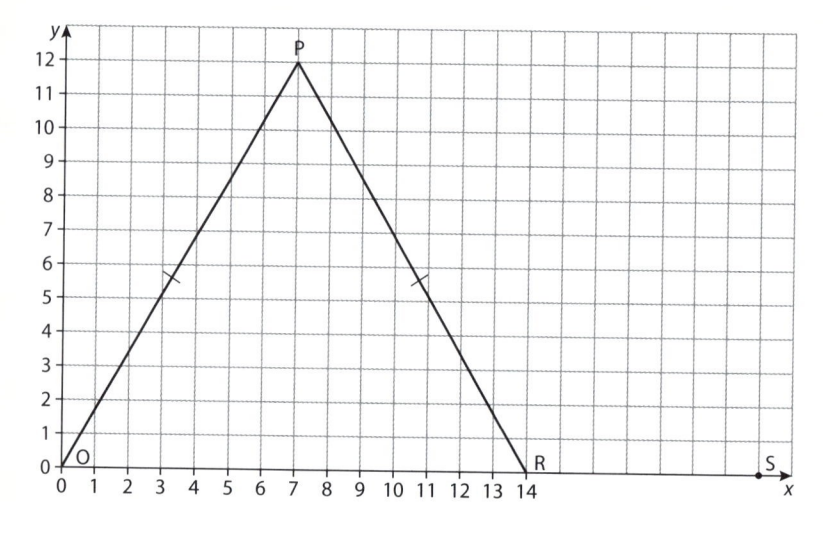

   ∠TRS =

(e) Calculate the size of the angle ∠PRO. ∠PRO =

   ⇒ ∠POR =
       ∠OPR =

3.

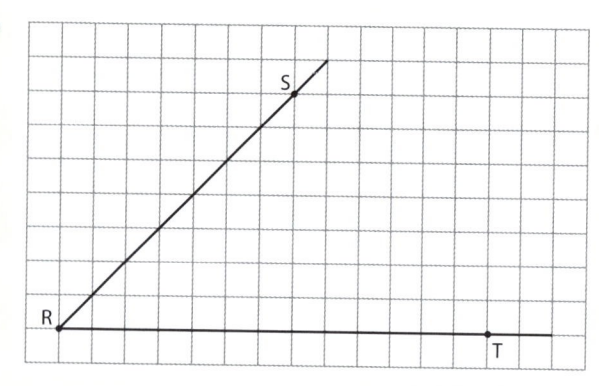

(a) Bisect the angle ∠RST using a compass and ruler. Name the bisector SU.

(b) Measure the angle ∠UST using a protractor.

   ∠UST =

Date .... Signed ....

4.

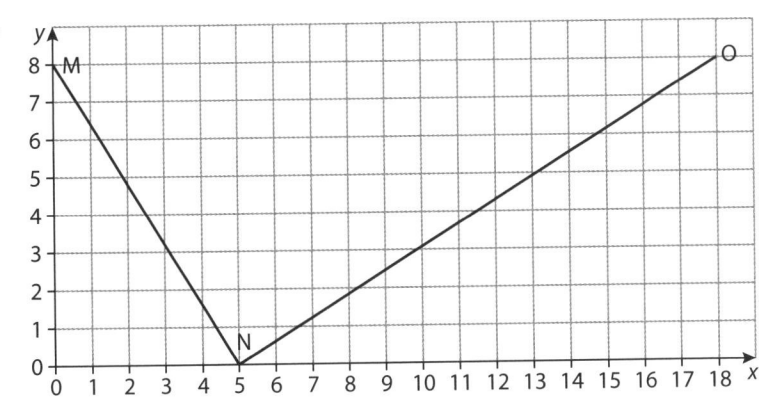

(a) Write down the co-ordinates of the points M =
   N =
   O =

(b) Bisect the line segment [MN] using only compass and straight edge.

(c) Bisect the line segment [NO] using only compass and straight edge.

(d) Find the coordinates of the point where the bisectors meet. Name this point P.

(e) Measure the lengths of the line segments (correct to the nearest mm).   [MP] =
   [NP] =
   [OP] =

5.

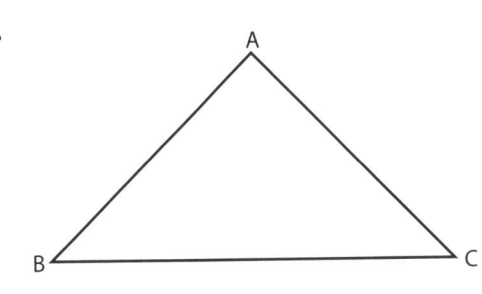

(a) Using a compass and straight edges, bisect the sides
   (i) AB   (ii) BC   (iii) CA.

(b) Name the point where the bisectors meet P

(c) Measure the length of the line segments.

   [AP] =
   [BP] =
   [CP] =

6.

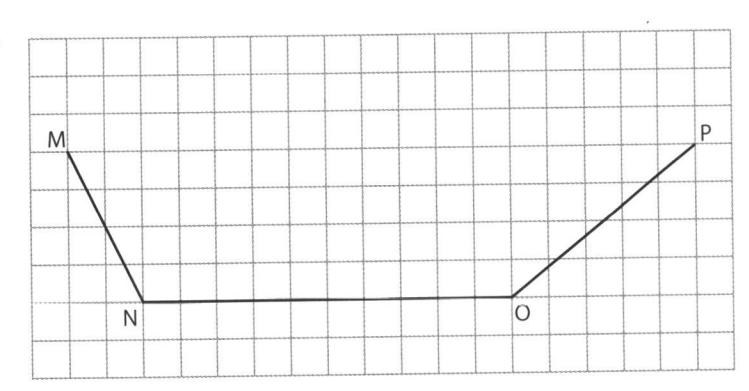

(a) Using a compass and ruler, draw the perpendicular bisectors of the line segments [MN], [NO] and [OP].

(b) Name the point of intersection of the bisectors of [MN] and [NO] R.
   Name the point of intersection of the bisectors of [NO] and [OP] S.

(c) Measure |RS|.

Date .... Signed ....

12.6 Geometry V

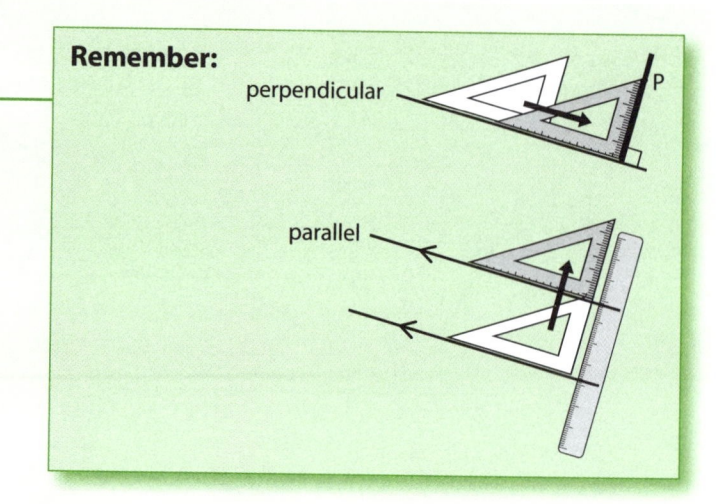

Remember:
perpendicular
parallel

1. Draw
   (i) a line *k*, drawn perpendicular to *l* through the point P,
   (ii) a line *m*, drawn parallel to *l* through P.

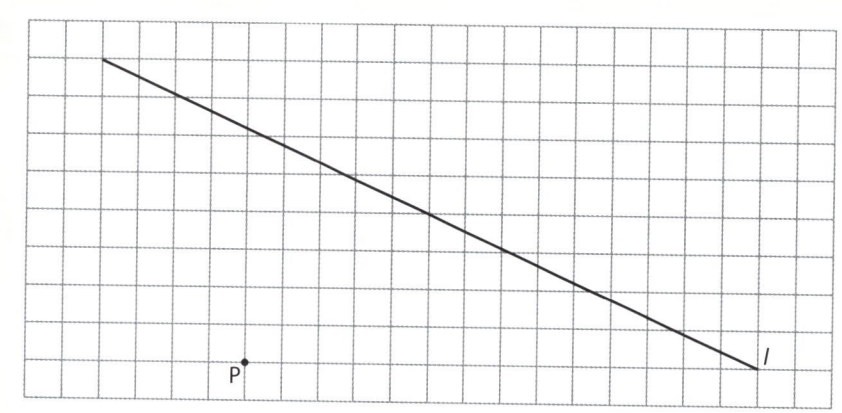

2. (a) Plot the points R(6, 2) and S(12, 4).
   (b) Draw the line RS.
   (c) Draw a line parallel to RS through the point T(6, 6).
   (d) Name the parallel line *a*.
   (e) Find the point where the line *a* crosses the *y*-axis.   (,   )

3. (a) Plot the points B(2, 1) and C(10, −2).
   (b) Draw a line through the points B and C.
   (c) Draw a line perpendicular to BC through the point D(3,5).
   (d) Draw a line perpendicular to BC through the point E(13, 2).
   (e) Draw a line parallel to BC through the point F(9, 5).
   (f) Calculate the area of the rectangle formed by these four lines.
   length =   cm
   width =   cm
   area =   cm²

Date ....   Signed ....

12.7 Geometry VI

1. Measure the length of each of the given line segments accurately, correct to the nearest millimetre.

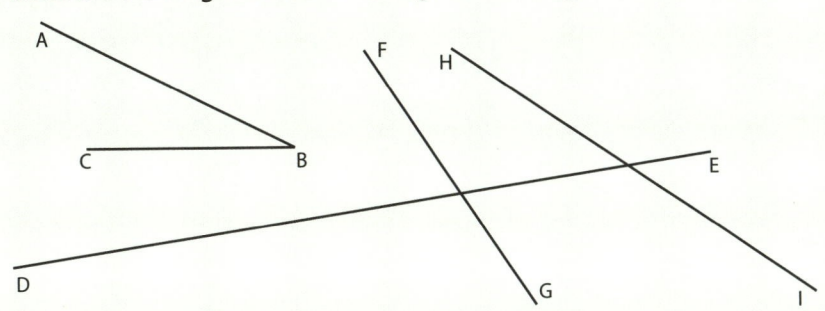

   |AB| =
   |BC| =
   |DE| =
   |FG| =
   |HI| =

2. (a) Using only a compass, straight edge and set square, divide each line segments into 2 equal segments. [Show all construction lines.]

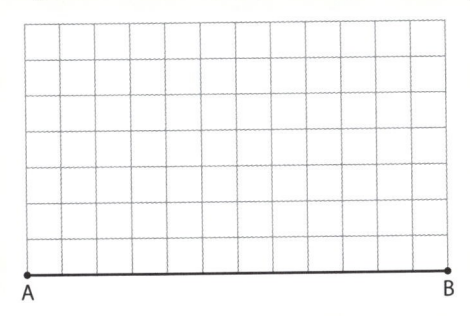

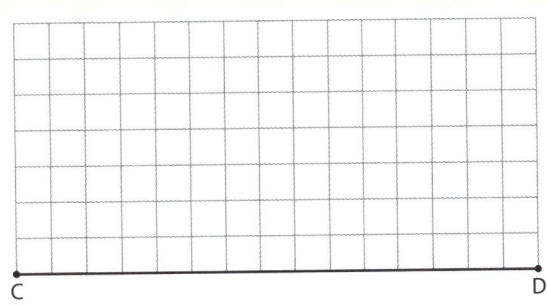

   (b) Check the accuracy of your construction by measuring the length of each segment and comparing their lengths to the total length.

   (i) |AB| =
   (ii) segment 1 =
   (iii) segment 2 =

   (i) |CD| =
   (ii) segment 1 =
   (iii) segment 2 =

3. (a) Using only a compass, straight edge and set square, divide each of the line segments [EF] and [GH] into 3 equal segments.

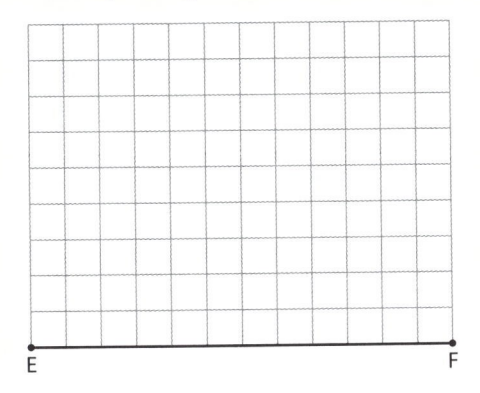

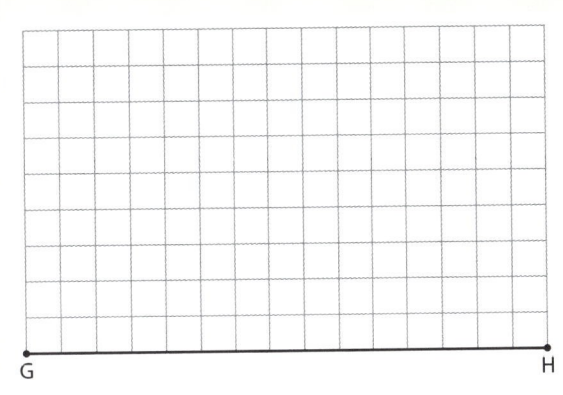

   (b) Check the accuracy of your construction by measuring the length of each segment and comparing their lengths to the total length.

   (i) |EF| =
   (ii) segment 1 =
   (iii) segment 2 =
   (iv) segment 3 =

   (i) |GH| =
   (ii) segment 1 =
   (iii) segment 2 =
   (iv) segment 3 =

   Date .... Signed ....

13.1 Algebra and Patterns

1. Study the following sequence of patterns. Complete the next two patterns and write a number sequence for each pattern set.

(a) number sequence   1, 2,   ,   ,

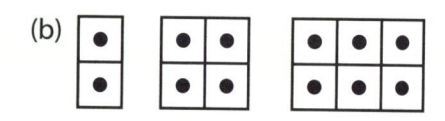

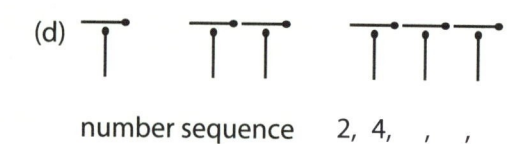

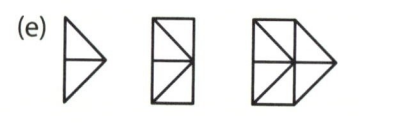

(b) number sequence   2, 4,   ,   ,

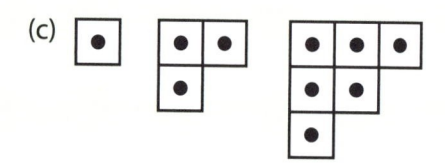

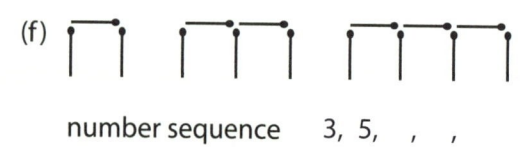

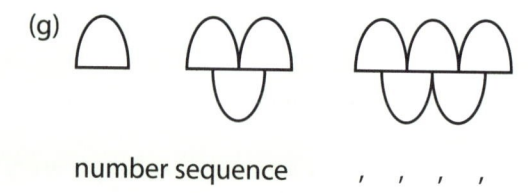

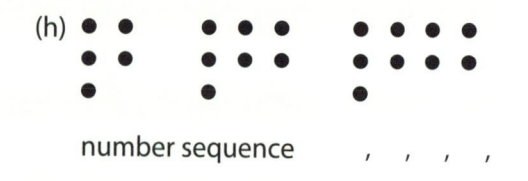

(c) number sequence   1, 3,   ,   ,

(d) number sequence   2, 4,   ,   ,

(e) number sequence   2, 4,   ,   ,

(f) number sequence   3, 5,   ,   ,

(g) number sequence   ,   ,   ,

(h) number sequence   ,   ,   ,

Date ....   Signed ....

2. Study each of the following sequences. Complete the pattern.
   (Hint: compare each sequence with the one above.)

	Term	1	2	3	4	5	10	20	30
(a)	Sequence	2	3	4					

	Term	1	2	3	4	5	10	20	30
(b)	Sequence	3	4	5					

	Term	1	2	3	4	5	10	20	30
(c)	Sequence	4	5	6					

	Term	1	2	3	4	5	10	20	30
(d)	Sequence	2	4	6					

	Term	1	2	3	4	5	10	20	30
(e)	Sequence	3	5	7					

	Term	1	2	3	4	5	10	20	30
(f)	Sequence	4	6	8					

	Term	1	2	3	4	5	10	20	30
(g)	Sequence	5	7	9					

	Term	1	2	3	4	5	10	20	30
(h)	Sequence	3	6	9					

	Term	1	2	3	4	5	10	20	30
(i)	Sequence	4	7	10					

	Term	1	2	3	4	5	10	20	30
(j)	Sequence	5	8	11					

	Term	1	2	3	4	5	10	20	30
(k)	Sequence	1	4	9					

	Term	1	2	3	4	5	10	20	30
(l)	Sequence	2	5	10					

	Term	1	2	3	4	5	10	20	30
(m)	Sequence	3	6	11					

Date .... Signed ....

3. Study the following triangles. Find the connection between the numbers at the vertices and the number in the centre and continue the pattern.

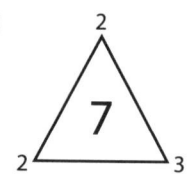

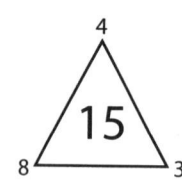

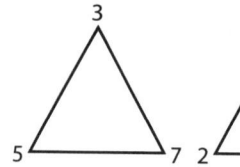

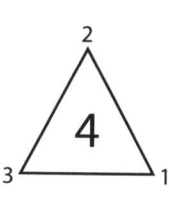

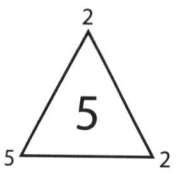

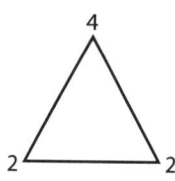

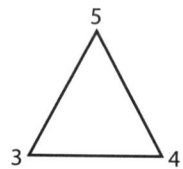

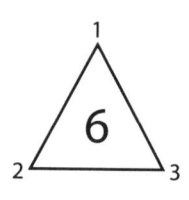

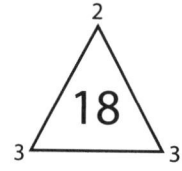

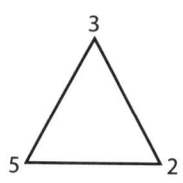

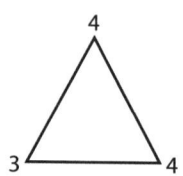

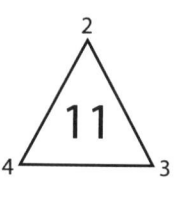

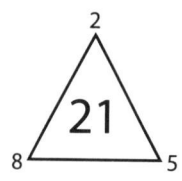

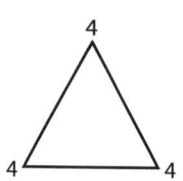

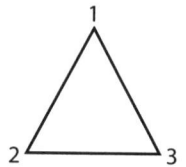

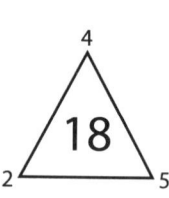

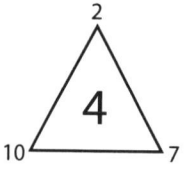

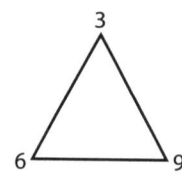

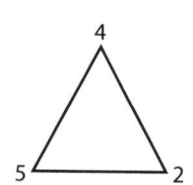

(a) 2,7,2,3 → 7; 2,6,1,3 → 6; 4,15,8,3 → 15; 3, _,5,7; 7, _,2,6

(b) 2,4,3,1 → 4; 3,4,3,2 → 4; 2,5,5,2 → 5; 4, _,2,2; 5, _,3,4

(c) 1,6,2,3 → 6; 2,16,2,4 → 16; 2,18,3,3 → 18; 3, _,5,2; 4, _,3,4

(d) 2,11,4,3 → 11; 3,19,5,4 → 19; 2,21,8,5 → 21; 4, _,4,4; 1, _,2,3

(e) 4,18,2,5 → 18; 3,8,1,3 → 8; 2,4,10,7 → 4; 3, _,6,9; 4, _,5,2

4. Study the circles below. Work out the number that should go into the centre of each circle.

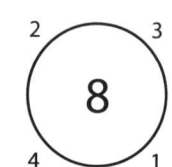

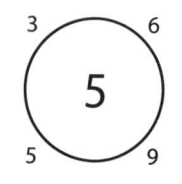

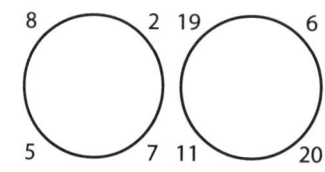

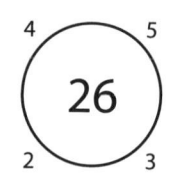

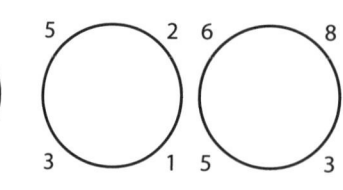

(a) 2,8,4,1 → 8; 3,9,5,6 → 9 ... etc.

(b) 4,26,2,3 → 26; 3,23,2,5 → 23; 5,39,4,6 → 39; ...

Date .... Signed ....

5. The following is a sequence of patterns made from matchsticks. In each case
   (a) draw the next two patterns in the sequence
   (b) complete the table showing the number of matchsticks needed for each pattern
   (c) find the number of matchsticks needed for the 8th, 10th and 20th pattern
   (d) describe in words how to find the number of matchsticks needed for the *n*th pattern.

(i)

Pattern	1	2	3	4	5	·······>	8	10	20
Number of matchsticks									

In words, how many matchsticks are needed for the *n*th pattern?

***

(ii)

Pattern	1	2	3	4	5	·······>	8	10	20
Number of matchsticks									

In words, how many matchsticks are needed for the *n*th pattern?

***

(iii)

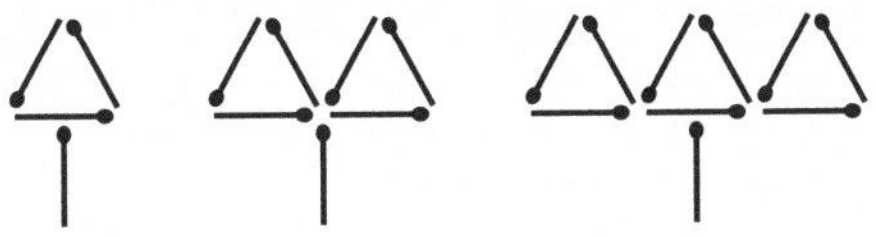

Pattern	1	2	3	4	5	·······>	8	10	20
Number of matchsticks									

In words, how many matchsticks are needed for the *n*th pattern?

***

(iv)

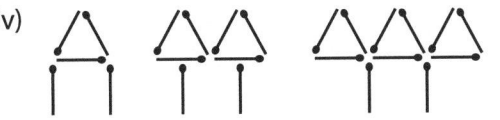

Pattern	1	2	3	4	5	·······>	8	10	20
Number of matchsticks									

In words, how many matchsticks are needed for the *n*th pattern?

***

Date ....   Signed ....

(v)

Pattern	1	2	3	4	5	·········>	8	10	20
Number of matchsticks									

In words, how many matchsticks are needed for the nth pattern?

***

(vi)

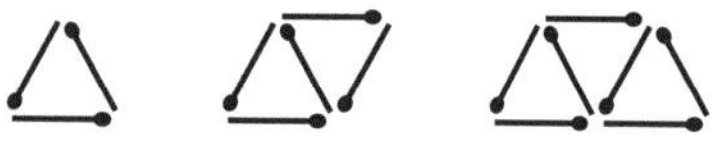

Pattern	1	2	3	4	5	·········>	8	10	20
Number of matchsticks									

In words, how many matchsticks are needed for the nth pattern?

***

(vii)

Pattern	1	2	3	4	5	·········>	8	10	20
Number of matchsticks									

In words, how many matchsticks are needed for the nth pattern?

***

(viii)

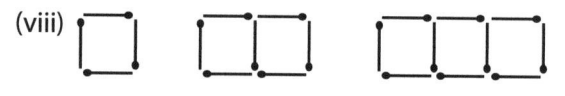

Pattern	1	2	3	4	5	·········>	8	10	20
Number of matchsticks									

In words, how many matchsticks are needed for the nth pattern?

***

Date .... Signed ....

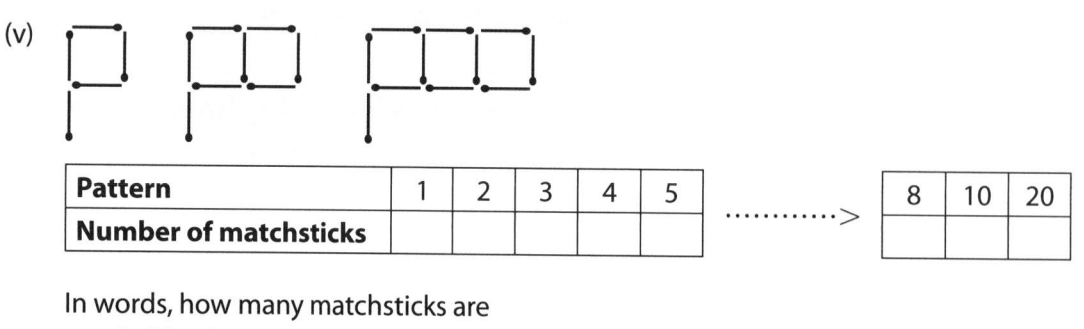

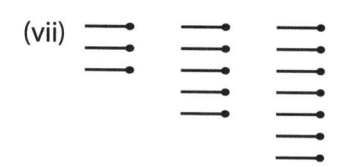

6. The following is a sequence of buildings each with a different number of storeys.

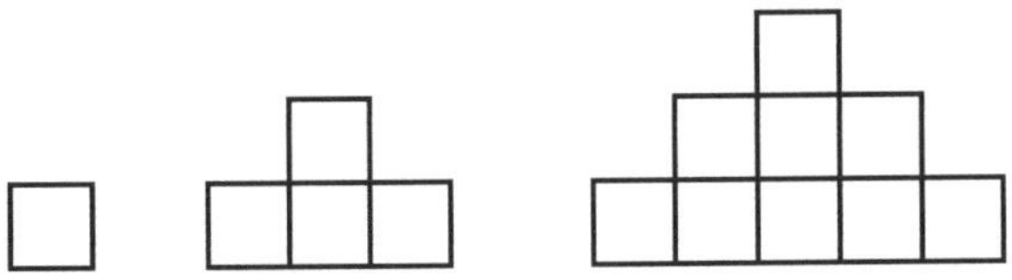

   (a) Using this pattern, draw the next 4-storey and 5-storey building.
   (b) Complete the following table.

Number of storeys	1	2	3	4	5
Number of blocks in bottom storey					
Total number of blocks per building					

	8	10	20

   ***

   In words, how many blocks are needed for the nth pattern?

7. Draw the next pattern in each of the following sequences and complete the tables.

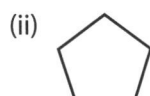

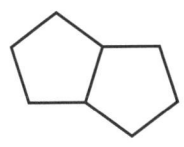

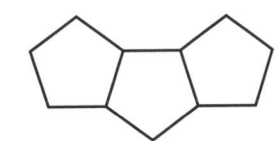

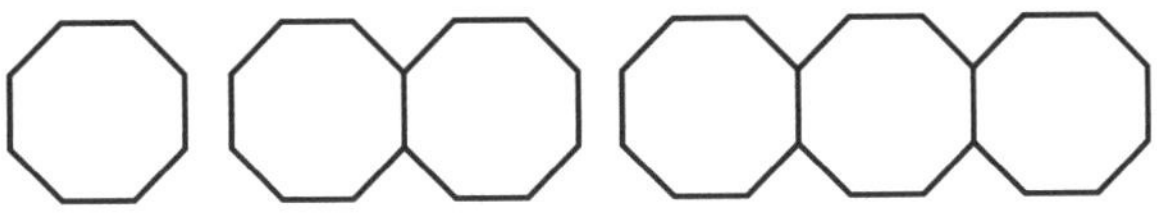

   (i)

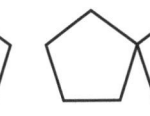

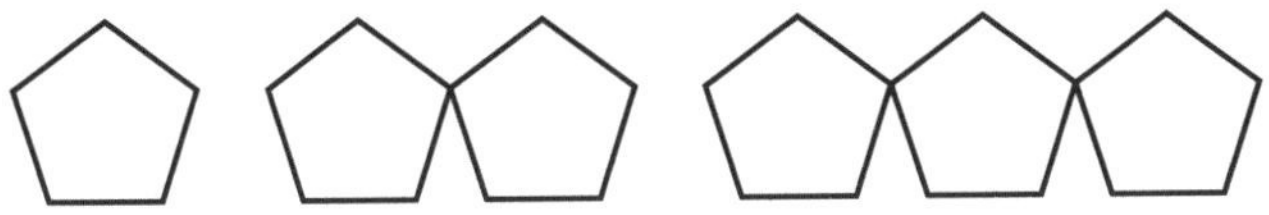

Pattern	1	2	3	4	5
Number of sticks needed					

	8	10	20

   (ii)

Pattern	1	2	3	4	5
Number of sticks needed					

	8	10	20

   (iii)

Pattern	1	2	3	4	5
Number of sticks needed					

	8	10	20

Date ....   Signed ....